Fundamentals

of the

Faith

Student Workbook

by David E. Sproule, II

Fundamentals of the Faith: Student Workbook

Copyright © 2015 by   David Sproule
4067 Leo Lane
Palm Beach Gardens, FL 33410

ISBN-10: 1518702880
ISBN-13: 978-1518702884

Table of Contents

Lesson 1: Authority in Religion

Fundamentals
of the Faith

I. **Authority Is _____ in _____ Matters of Life!**
   A. Having authority is a necessity of life – in a home, school, nation, religion, etc.
      1. Authority is "the right to command and enforce obedience; the power to give orders."
      2. While some individuals may reject or despise authority, that does not diminish the need for authority in all matters of life. In fact, it may intensify the need.
   B. Authority makes the difference between harmonious unity and chaotic confusion.
      1. Imagine the stock exchange without an authoritative standard of currency.
      2. Imagine the produce market without an authoritative standard of weights.
      3. Imagine the lumber yard without an authoritative standard of measurements.
      4. Imagine the football field without an authoritative standard of rules.
      5. Imagine the military unit without an authoritative standard of regulations.
   C. Nowhere else is authority as essential as it is in _____.
      1. An objective standard is absolutely crucial when it comes to our eternal salvation!
      2. Without authority in religion, then division, chaos and confusion will exist.
      3. The condition of the religious world today reflects a lack of following a standard.
      4. Religious unity is only possible by submitting to the same standard of authority.
      5. It is imperative that we find and follow that standard of authority.
   D. Jesus taught that there are only _____ (Matt 21:23-27).
      1. One source of authority is from Heaven, the other is from Men.
      2. That which is authorized by heaven must be believed and obeyed.
      3. That which is authorized merely by men must be rejected and not obeyed.
      4. It is imperative that we differentiate between the two and yield to heaven's authority.

II. **Man Has Failed in Many Attempts to Identify _____ in Religion!**
   A. Man has sought "_____" for an adequate source of authority:
      1. Follow the majority (Ex. 23:2; Gen. 6:5-13; 1 Sam. 8:4-8; Matt. 7:13-14).
      2. Follow a group of men—church councils, synods, conferences, associations (Gal. 1:9).
      3. Follow a man—like the Pope or a favorite preacher (Eph. 1:22-23; Gal. 1:6-9).
      4. Follow human traditions/commandments of men (cf. Mt. 15:3-9; Mk. 7:1-13; Col. 2:8).
      5. Follow human creeds—confessions of faith, manuals and church disciplines (Gal. 1:9).
      6. Follow the religious beliefs of our ancestors (Phil. 3:3-14; Matt. 10:37).
      7. There is no adequate human external source of authority in religion.
   B. Man has sought "_____" for an adequate source of authority:
      1. Personal feelings (Prov. 14:12; 28:26; Jer. 10:23).
      2. Individual conscience & sincerity (Acts 23:1; 26:9-11; 1 Tim. 1:13-16; 4:2; Mt. 7:21-23).
      3. Human wisdom & reasoning (Isa. 55:8-9; 1 Cor. 1:18-29; 2 Kgs. 5:11; 2 Sam. 6:3-7).
      4. Direct (modern-day) revelation from God (2 Pet. 2:1; 1 John 4:1; Jude 3).
      5. There is no adequate human internal source of authority in religion.
   C. Neither man nor any of his devices are an adequate authority in religion.
      1. "There is a way that seems right to a man, but its end is the way of death" (Pro. 14:12).
      2. "...It is not in man who walks to direct his own steps" (Jer. 10:23).
      3. Man's ways and devices lead him "far from God," not toward Him (Matt. 15:8-9).
      4. For Jesus taught, "If the blind leads the blind, both will fall into a ditch" (Matt. 15:14).

III. _____ **Has All Authority in Religious Matters!**

   A. The only authority in religion is the authority of _____, of _____!!!
      1. "God made the world and everything in it...He is Lord of heaven and earth" (Ac. 17:24).
      2. All authority inherently resides in God the Father (Gen. 1-3; Rom. 9:8-24).
      3. God has spoken His Word through His Son (Heb. 1:1-2).

   B. _____ was given by the Father unto _____!
      1. Christ has all authority in heaven and on earth (Matt. 28:18).
      2. Christ is the head/authority over all, including His church (Eph. 1:20-23; Col. 1:18).
      3. Christ is to be heard in all things and over all persons (Matt. 17:1-5; Acts 3:22-23).
      4. Consequences are assured upon those who do not heed His words (Acts 3:22-23).
      5. Those who heard Christ speak recognized His inherent authority (Matt. 7:28-29).

   C. Christ's authority resides in _____!
      1. The authoritative words He spoke were from the Father (Heb. 1:1-2).
        (a) "For I have not spoken on My own authority; but the Father who sent Me gave Me a command, what I should say and what I should speak" (John 12:49).
        (b) "Whatever I speak, just as the Father has told Me, so I speak" (John 12:50).
      2. The authoritative words He spoke will judge all mankind (John 12:48).
        (a) "...The word that I have spoken will judge him in the last day."
      3. When we understand where all authority resides, we know also where it is not.

   D. Christ delivered His all-authoritative Word to His _____ through the _____!
      1. While with His apostles, He gave them the words of the Father (John 17:8, 14).
      2. When Jesus left the earth, He sent the Holy Spirit to the apostles. The Spirit:
        (a) Would "teach [the apostles] all things" (John 14:26).
        (b) Would "bring to [the apostles'] remembrance all things [Jesus] said" (14:26).
        (c) Would "guide [the apostles] into all truth" (John 16:13, 7-15).
        (d) Would "speak" through the apostles (Mark 13:11).
        (e) Like Christ, would speak the words and will of the Father (John 16:13).

   E. The apostles spoke and wrote by inspiration of the Holy Spirit!
      1. The writings of the Old Testament and New Testament:
        (a) Never came by "any private interpretation" of the writer (2 Pet. 1:20).
        (b) Never "came by the will of man" (2 Pet. 1:21).
        (c) Were the result of inspired men being "moved by the Holy Spirit" (2 Pet. 1:21).
        (d) Were the result of "the inspiration of God" (i.e., "God-breathed") (2 Tim. 3:16).
        (e) Are "the Word of God" and not "the word of men" (1 Thess. 2:13).
        (f) Are "the commandments of the Lord" and not man (1 Cor. 14:37).
      2. The inspired writings reveal to us the mind and will of God (1 Cor. 2:11-13).
      3. Scripture was given so that man might have the writers' understanding (Eph. 3:3-5).

   F. Thus, the very authority of God is inherent in the _____!
      1. The inspired words are preserved in the Bible, providing us with Heaven's authority.
      2. The same word that the Father gave to the Son and that the Holy Spirit received and gave to the apostles is the same word that is written in the Bible! It is God's Word!
      3. The Bible alone is the true objective standard in religious matters today.
      4. God authorizes only the teachings and practices found in the New Testament.
      5. Any teaching or practice foreign or contrary to the N.T. is not authorized by God.
      6. Our utmost attention must be given to learning and following His authoritative Word!

G. God's written word is the only authority that can prepare us for judgment and eternity!
   1. On the day of judgment, every person will stand before Christ (Ro. 14:10; 2 Cor. 5:10).
   2. On the day of judgment, Christ Himself will be the Judge of all (Acts 17:30-31).
   3. Christ will use His Word to judge all mankind on the last day (John 12:48).
   4. Each one will be "judged according to their works" by the words of Christ (Rev. 20:12).
   5. No human standard will be present on the day of judgment.
   6. No human standard will determine man's eternal destiny.
   7. Only Christ's all-authoritative Word will judge and determine eternal destinies.

IV. **The All-Authoritative Word of God Is _____ and _____!**
   A. God's Word is all-sufficient – it is complete and lacking in nothing.
      1. "All Scripture is given by the inspiration of God" (2 Tim. 3:16).
      2. With it, man is "complete, thoroughly equipped for every good work" (2 Tim. 3:16-17).
      3. With it, man has "all things that pertain to life and godliness" (2 Pet. 1:3).
      4. To impugn the all-sufficiency of Scripture would be to impugn the wisdom of God.
   B. God's Word is all-delivered – it has all been given and there is nothing else to be given.
      1. God's will for man has been "once for all delivered to the saints" (Jude 3).
      2. No further revelation has been, will be or even needs to be given. It is final!
      3. To claim direct revelation today is to charge God with lying and falsehood!
   C. God's Word is all that is needed to preach the fullness of the gospel!
      1. There is "not another" gospel, except one that has been "perverted" (Gal. 1:6-7).
      2. There is not "any other gospel" that can be or should be preached (Gal. 1:8-9).
      3. For anyone who preaches anything more, less or different than the revealed gospel, God has pronounced a curse: "Let him be accursed" (Gal. 1:8-9).
   D. God's Word is "the perfect law of liberty" (Jas. 1:25).
      1. The word "perfect" emphasizes that it is without defect and all-sufficient to accomplish its purpose.
      2. God's "perfect law" requires man's compliance and not defiance (Jas. 1:21-25).

V. **Man's Only Proper Response Is to _____ the All-Authoritative Word!**
   A. We must accept God's will completely (Luke 10:16; John 12:48).
   B. We must, like the Bereans, "search the Scriptures" as our standard (Acts 17:11).
   C. We must do all things by the name/authority of Christ (Col. 3:17).
   D. We must recognize that "there is no other name under heaven given among men by which we must be saved" (Acts 4:12).
   E. We must "walk by faith," by walking according to His Word (2 Cor. 5:7; Rom. 10:17).
   F. We must demonstrate our love for Him by keeping His commandments (John 14:15).
   G. We must not add to or subtract from God's Word (Deut. 4:2; 12:32; Rev. 22:18-19).
      1. "God will add" eternal punishment to those who add to His word (Rev. 22:18).
      2. "God shall take away" eternal reward from those who take away from His Word (22:19).
   H. We must not modify, substitute or pervert the will of God (Gal. 1:6-9; Matt. 15:3, 9).
      1. Those who elevate their own doctrines, ideas and traditions above God's Word:
         (a) "Lay aside the commandment of God" (Mark 7:8).
         (b) "Reject the commandment of God" (Mark 7:9).
         (c) "Make the word of God of no effect" (Mark 7:13).
      2. As a consequence, "Every plant which [the] heavenly Father has not planted will be uprooted" (Matt. 15:13).

I.   We must not go beyond that which is written (1 Cor. 4:6).
   1.   "Whoever transgresses [goes too far, NASB] and does not abide in the doctrine of Christ does not have God" (2 John 9).
J.   We must not speak beyond that which is written (1 Pet. 4:11).
K.   We must hear Christ's Words and prepare for judgment (Matt. 17:5; John 12:48).
L.   We must respect and obey God's Word to enter heaven (Matt. 7:21-27; Heb. 5:9).
   1.   Jesus' words in Matthew 7:21 are key: "Not everyone who says to Me, 'Lord, Lord,' shall enter the kingdom of heaven, but he who does the will of My Father in heaven."

VI. **God Will _____ That Which Is _____!**
A.   Whatever is not _____ by God is not _____ to God, even if "intended to be."
   1.   Cain's worship (surely intended to be acceptable) was not acceptable to God (Gen. 4).
   2.   Israel's worship was not acceptable to God (Mal. 1:6-9).
   3.   The worship of the Pharisees and scribes was not acceptable to God (Matt. 15:7-9).
   4.   Uzzah's "well-intentioned" touching of the Ark was not acceptable (2 Sam. 6:3-7).
   5.   Moses' striking of the rock rather than speaking was not acceptable (Num. 20:7-12)
   6.   When men do not respect and obey God's authority, disastrous consequences await.
B.   The Bible often uses the word "strange" in the sense of "not authorized by God."
   1.   Nadab and Abihu offered "strange" fire, not authorized by God (Lev. 10:1-3).
   2.   "King Solomon loved many strange women," not authorized by God (1 Kgs. 11:1).
   3.   Israel did evil against God "in marrying strange women," not authorized (Neh. 13:27).
   4.   Sodom & Gomorrah had "gone after strange flesh," not authorized by God (Jude 7).
   5.   We are warned about being "carried about with...strange doctrines" (Heb. 13:9).
   6.   When men pursue that which is "strange" to God's authority, destruction awaits.
C.   Eternal condemnation awaits anyone who disregards the authority of God's Word.
   1.   "And then I will declare to them, I never knew you; depart from Me, you who practice lawlessness!'" (Matt. 7:23).
   2.   "These shall be punished with everlasting destruction from the presence of the Lord and from the glory of His power" (2 Thess. 1:8-9).

VII. **Conclusion**
A.   Man must recognize his own inferiority before God (Isa. 55:7-8).
B.   Man must look to Christ and His Word for authority in all religious matters (Col. 3:17).
C.   Man must learn to "Speak where the Bible speaks" (1 Pet. 4:11).
   1.   Man must learn to "Be silent where the Bible is silent."
   2.   Man must learn to "Call Bible things by Bible names."
   3.   Man must learn to "Do Bible things in Bible ways."
   4.   For the Bible alone is our standard in all things!
D.   Man must live his life and prepare for the day of judgment by realizing that:
   1.   Jesus respected God's authority, limited Himself to it and obeyed (Jn. 6:38; 12:49-50).
   2.   The Holy Spirit respected God's authority, limited Himself to it and obeyed (Jn. 16:13).
   3.   The apostles were to respect God's authority, limit themselves to it and obey (Gal. 1:8).
   4.   The angels were to respect God's authority, limit themselves to it and obey (Gal. 1:8).
   5.   Therefore, we all must respect God's authority, limit ourselves to it and obey (Mt. 7:21).
E.   There are only two possible sources of authority (Matt 21:23-27).
   1.   One source of authority is from Heaven, the other is from Men.
   2.   That which is authorized by heaven must be believed and obeyed.
   3.   That which is authorized merely by men must be rejected and not obeyed.
   4.   "We must obey God rather than men" (Acts 5:29).

Lesson 2: The Two Covenants

Fundamentals *of the* Faith

I. **The Bible Is Divided into _____.**
   A. A covenant is an agreement between two parties.
      1. The agreement involves specified conditions and promised benefits.
      2. Once accepted, both parties are obligated to fulfill their stated requirements.
   B. In the Bible, God established covenants.
      1. As for God, He was the one who set the conditions/terms of the covenants.
      2. As for man, he could accept or reject the terms set out by God (but not alter them).
      3. God is the one to make the demands; man is the one to submit and follow them.
      4. God cannot (and does not) break His side of the agreement.
      5. Man must fulfill his side of the covenant, in order to receive the promised benefits.
   C. The Bible contains two main covenants that God made: an old covenant and a new covenant.
      1. The Old Covenant was made between God and a nation (Israel).
      2. The New Covenant was/is made between God and individuals (Christians).
      3. True to the word "covenant," each covenant had specified conditions and promised benefits.
   D. A major key to Bible study is understanding and applying the proper distinction between "_____" and "_____."
      1. Failing to make that distinction has led to much religious confusion today.
      2. Failing to make that distinction has led and will lead many souls to be lost.
      3. God makes a distinction between the Old and the New, and we must follow it.

II. **God Established _____.**
   A. The first covenant was made by God with _____.
      1. "I have made a covenant with you and with Israel" (Ex. 34:27).
   B. The first covenant was made by God with the Israelites when they came out of Egypt.
      1. "...After the children of Israel had gone out of the land of Egypt...the Lord called to him from the mountain, saying, '...Now therefore, if you will indeed obey My voice and keep My covenant, then you shall be a special treasure to Me above all people...And you shall be to Me a kingdom of priests and a holy nation.'...Then all the people answered together and said, 'All that the Lord has spoken we will do'" (Ex. 19:1-8; cf. 24:1-8).
   C. The first covenant was made by God with the Israelites at Mt. Sinai
      1. "The Lord our God made a covenant with us in Horeb" (Deut. 5:2).
      2. God came down "on Mount Sinai, and spoke with them from heaven, and gave them just ordinances and true laws, good statutes and commandments" (Neh. 9:13).
   D. The first covenant was made by God with the Israelites and only with the Israelites.
      1. It was a national law, which did not include any other nation but the Jews.
      2. "And God spoke all these words, saying: 'I am the Lord your God, who brought you out of the land of Egypt, out of the house of bondage'" (Ex. 20:1-2).
      3. "...It is a sign between Me and you throughout your generations...It is a sign between Me and the children of Israel forever" (Ex. 31:12-17).
      4. "For what great nation is there that has God so near to it...? And what great nation is there that has such statutes and righteous judgments...?" (Deut. 4:7-8).

III. God Intended the First Covenant to Be _____.

A. As a national law and covenant, limited only to the Jews, it should have been obvious that it was only temporary.
1. For, God had made a covenant with Abraham, promising, "In your seed all the nations of the earth shall be blessed" (Gen. 22:18).
2. God promised to make Abraham "a great nation" (Gen. 12:1-3), and so He did with the Israelite nation. (God changed the name of Abraham's grandson, Jacob, to Israel.)
3. But, His ultimate promise was a blessing to "all the families (or nations) of the earth" (Gen. 12:3; 22:18). This could not be and was not fulfilled in the single nation of Israel.

B. God foretold through Jeremiah that He would establish a new covenant.
1. "The days are coming, says the Lord, when I will make a new covenant" (Jer. 31:31).
2. The Hebrews writer quoted this passage in Hebrews 8:6-13 to show:
    (a) The new covenant was "a better covenant...established on better promises" (8:6).
    (b) The covenant with Israel was the "first covenant" (8:7), which implies a second.
    (c) The "new covenant...made the first obsolete...ready to vanish away" (8:13).
3. The Divine plan for a "new covenant" indicated the "first covenant" was temporary.

C. More than 1,000 years before Jeremiah, God had foretold of Judah's role in His plan.
1. "The scepter shall not depart from Judah, Nor a lawgiver from between his feet, Until Shiloh comes; And to Him shall be the obedience of the people" (Gen. 49:10).
2. The Messiah (Christ) would come through the tribe of Judah, the kingly tribe.
    (a) However, the Messiah (Christ) would come as a priest (Zech. 6:13).
    (b) And, the priests of the covenant with Israel came from Levi (Num. 3:6-8).
3. Therefore, "For the priesthood being changed, of necessity there is also a change of the law" (Heb. 7:12).
    (a) Jesus could not be a priest on the earth, being from the tribe of Judah (Heb. 8:4).
    (b) Therefore, for the Messiah (from the tribe of Judah) to serve as priest, it required a change of the covenant.
    (c) For Jesus to be our "merciful and faithful High Priest" today (Heb. 2:17-18), we cannot be bound by (or seek to go back to) that old covenant.

D. God's original design for the first covenant was for it to be temporary, "till the Seed should come to whom the promise was made" (Gal. 3:19).
1. It was "added because of transgressions" (Gal. 3:19).
2. It was given that sin "might appear sin" and "exceedingly sinful" (Rom. 7:13).
3. It was designed to bring about fulfillment of the promise to Abraham (Gal. 3:16-19).
4. It was purposed to be the "tutor to bring us to Christ" (Gal. 3:24).
5. It served as "a shadow of the good things to come" (Heb. 10:1).

IV. God Intentionally _____ **of the First Covenant.**

A. God affirmed that "it was weak through the flesh" (Rom. 8:3), that it was annulled "because of its weakness" (Heb. 7:18) and because it was not "faultless" (Heb. 8:7).
1. That does not mean that God was weak or ineffectual in making such a covenant.
2. Nor does it mean that God messed up the first covenant but got it right on the second.
3. The design of the first covenant was exactly what God intended, in order to prepare all of mankind for the "better" and "everlasting covenant" (Heb. 8:6; 13:20).

B. It was limited/weak/faulty in that:
1. It was made with only one nation (Ex. 19:1-8; Deut. 5:1-6).
2. It could not remove sin (Heb. 9:12-14; 10:1-4).
3. It could not justify (Gal. 3:11; Acts 13:39), give righteousness (2:21) or give life (3:21).

4. It could not make one perfect (Heb. 7:19).
    C. If the first had been perfect, then there would have been no need for the second or for the Savior, Redeemer and Sacrificial Lamb of the second (Heb. 8:7).
    D. God knew what He was doing!
V. **God _____ the First Covenant Himself, in Order to _____ the Second.**
    A. God promised that He was going to make a new covenant (Jer. 31:31-34).
    B. The old covenant was intended to last "till the Seed should come to whom the promise was made" (Gal. 3:19), and that Seed "is Christ" (Gal. 3:16).
        1. Therefore, the coming of Christ signaled the ending of the old covenant.
    C. Jesus declared that He came to "fulfill" the covenant that God made with Israel, and that it would "pass" when "all [the law] is fulfilled" (Matt. 5:17-18).
        1. As He died, Jesus declared, "It is finished" (John 19:30).
        2. After His death and resurrection, Jesus then declared that all things had been "fulfilled" (Luke 24:44).
        3. If all the covenant had been fulfilled, then the covenant was to pass away.
    D. The N.T. makes it clear that the first covenant was "taken away in Christ" (2 Cor. 3:14).
        1. Three times in this same passage of 2 Corinthians 3 it is affirmed that the first covenant "was passing away" (3:7, 11, 13).
    E. The removal of the covenant took place in the _____.
        1. He "has broken down the middle wall of separation, having abolished in His flesh the enmity, that is, the law of commandments contained in ordinances...through the cross, thereby putting to death the enmity" (Eph. 2:14-16).
        2. He "wiped out the handwriting of requirements that was against us, which was contrary to us. And He has taken it out of the way, having nailed it to the cross" (Col. 2:14).
    F. The removal of the covenant included _____. (See also VII in Lesson 8.)
        1. Some have tried to divide the O.T. into a "moral law" and "ceremonial law."
            (a) They want, essentially, the Ten Commandments to be the "moral law," and the rest of the Old Testament to be the "ceremonial law."
            (b) Then, they claim that the "ceremonial law" (with the animal sacrifices, feast days, etc.) was taken away by Christ, but the "moral law" is still binding.
            (c) They want the Ten Commandments, including the Sabbath, still in effect today.
        2. The Ten Commandments were part of the covenant that God made with Israel at Mt. Sinai (Ex. 34:27-28; Deut. 4:13; 9:9-11; 1 Kgs. 8:9, 21).
        3. The Ten Commandments, along with all the O.T. law, were abrogated in Christ.
            (a) We are "dead to" and "delivered from" the law which included, "You shall not covet" (Rom. 7:1-7)—i.e., the Ten Commandments.
            (b) We are no longer subject to the law which included the "Sabbaths" (Col. 2:14-17)—i.e., the Ten Commandments.
            (c) We are no longer under any portion of the law that was "written and engraved on stones" (2 Cor. 3:3-18)—i.e., the Ten Commandments.
    G. There are entire books in the New Testament that have as their overriding theme the abrogation of the Old Testament (including Romans, Galatians and Hebrews).
        1. The book of Romans clearly teaches that the old covenant has been removed.
        2. We are "not under law" (6:15), "have been delivered from the law" (7:6), are "free from that law" (7:3; 8:2), and are "dead to the law through the body of Christ" (7:4).

VI. God Established _____.

A. At the same moment the first was removed (in the death of Christ on the cross, Eph. 2), God's second covenant came in force.
 1. "He is the Mediator of the new covenant, by means of death" (Heb. 9:15).
 2. "For where there is a testament, there must also of necessity be the death of the testator. For a testament is in force after men are dead, since it has no power at all while the testator lives" (Heb. 9:16-17).
 3. Jesus tied the shedding of His blood with "the new covenant" (Matt. 26:28).
B. The first had to be removed for the second to be established.
 1. Jesus is the "Mediator of a better covenant" (Heb. 8:6).
 2. "He takes away the first that He may establish the second" (Heb. 10:9-10).
C. The second covenant, the New Testament:
 1. Is the fulfillment of the promise made to Abraham (Gen. 12:1-3; 22:18; Gal. 3:13-24).
 2. Is for all people (Acts 3:25; Mark 16:15-16; Luke 24:44-47; Heb. 2:9).
 3. Is effected by the blood of Jesus (Heb. 5:8-9; 9:12-28; 10:1-4, 29; Matt. 26:28).
 4. Completely removes sin (Heb. 8:12; 9:25; Col. 2:11; Rev. 1:5).
 5. Sanctifies and justifies (Heb. 9:13-14; 10:10-14, 29; 13:12; Rom. 10:9; Gal. 3:24).
 6. Gives life and makes perfect (Rom. 8:2; Heb. 9:11; 10:14).
 7. Is to last until the end of time (Heb. 13:20; Rev. 14:6).

VII. While Christians Are Not Under the Old Covenant, It Still Has _____.

A. The Old Testament is no longer binding today, but that does not mean it is worthless.
B. Jesus and the New Testament writers must have seen its value, for they all used it.
C. We have the Old Testament "for our learning" & "admonition" (Rom. 15:4; 1 Cor. 10:11).
 1. We learn about the origin of all things, including man and the universe (Gen. 1:1-31).
 2. We learn about the deity of Jesus (Acts 2:22-36; 3:13-26; 10:43; 17:3; Luke 24:27, 44).
 3. We learn about the church (2 Sam. 7:11-16; Isa. 2:1-4; Dan. 2:44; Micah 4:1-5).
 4. We are presented with a shadow of Christianity (Col. 2:16-17; Heb. 8:5; 10:1).
 5. We see Jesus as the scapegoat, the Passover lamb, the high priest, the brass serpent.
 6. We read background on people like Abraham, Elijah, Moses, David, Job, Naaman, etc.
 7. We read background on events like Lot's wife, Esau's birthright, Elijah's praying, etc.
 8. We read background on days like the Passover, Pentecost, Sabbath, etc.
 9. We connect Noah's flood to baptism, Jonah to the resurrection, Canaan to heaven, etc.
 10. We gain foundational knowledge on sin, faith, righteousness, holiness, prayer, etc.
 11. We gain insight into the heart of God and His longings for the heart of man.
 12. We come to know God more personally and deeply.
D. Much of the New Testament is better understood with a knowledge of the Old Testament.
E. It has been said, "The Old Testament is the New Testament concealed, and the New Testament is the Old Testament revealed."

VIII. Conclusion

A. The Bible student must recognize the distinction between the O.T. and the N.T.
B. Some denominational errors have originated and lingered in the improper usage and reliance on Old Testament law for justification of doctrines and practices.
C. The Old Testament is no longer a binding law on us today.
D. The Old Testament was removed at the same time that the New Testament began.
E. To attempt to be justified by the Old Testament today is to "fall from grace" (Gal. 5:4).
F. The New Testament beautifully reveals God's full plan for man's redemption through the sacrificial gift of His Son and the message of His gospel.

Lesson 3: The Divine Origin of the Church

I. Having Knowledge about the _____ of Anything Is Desired and Important.
   A. When we meet someone, we like to know, "Where are you from?"
   B. When we buy a product, we may want to know, "Was this made in the U.S.A.?"
   C. When we buy produce, we may want to know, "Was this grown locally?"
   D. We want to know about the origin, because that usually provides very helpful information about the thing being studied or considered.
   E. Knowing "where someone/something came from" will usually tell us volumes; in fact, it will often tell us all that we need to know.

II. Knowing the _____ Will Help Us to Understand It Tremendously.
   A. "Where did the church come from? When did it start? Who started it?"
      1. These are questions that need answers, if we are going to understand the church and make a proper evaluation of it.
   B. There is great confusion today about the church, and much of it stems from:
      1. A lack of knowledge about the Divine origin of the church.
      2. A lack of knowledge about the Divine nature of the church.
      3. A lack of knowledge about the Divine identity of the church.
      4. Years of exposure to man-made religion, with no concept of anything else.
      5. Assumption that denominationalism is "the norm."
      6. These matters will be addressed in these next three lessons.
   C. Was man responsible for the establishment and beginning of the church?
      1. If so, then the church can be nothing more than a glorified social club or association.
   D. Was God responsible for the establishment and beginning of the church?
      1. If so, then the church is among the greatest institutions ever created.
      2. If so, then man would be foolish to dismiss the church as insignificant or unnecessary.
      3. If so, then we must investigate the church and give it our utmost attention.
   E. Since we read about the church in the Bible, then the Bible is our sole source of information and direction.

III. The Church of the Bible Was _____ from Eternity.
   A. The Bible teaches that the church was "in accordance with the _____ which [God] carried out in Christ Jesus our Lord" (Eph. 3:10-11, NASB).
      1. The church was a part of God's "purpose" from before the ages of time.
      2. "Before the mountains were brought forth, Or ever You had formed the earth and the world, Even from everlasting to everlasting, You are God" (Psa. 90:2).
      3. That's "when" God purposed the church—before creation.
   B. We need to understand that God had a plan/purpose in place "from everlasting."
      1. The church was part of His eternal plan.
      2. God planned/purposed for man to have the opportunity to be "in Christ," and He planned for this "before the foundation of the world" (Eph. 1:4).
      3. God planned/purposed to save and extend grace "to us in Christ Jesus," and He planned for this "before time began" (2 Tim. 1:9).
      4. God planned/purposed to redeem us "with the precious blood of Christ," and He "foreordained" this "before the foundation of the world" (1 Pet. 1:18-20; Rev. 13:8).
      5. In like manner, the church was integral to God's eternal saving plan (Eph. 3:10-11).

C. The church was not a last-minute thought, addition or change to the unfolding of God's plan through the progression of time.
   1. The church was not established because the Jews rejected God's kingdom.
   2. The church was not established as a "parenthesis," until Jesus would return to establish His kingdom.
   3. The church was not established by man.
D. The church was established according to the eternal purpose of God!

IV. The Church of the Bible Was _____.
  A. The prophet _____ foretold the establishment of God's church.
    1. By "God in heaven," Daniel interpreted a dream of King Nebuchadnezzar in Daniel 2.
    2. The interpretation of the dream foretold of four successive world empires:
      (a) The Babylonian Empire (606-539 B.C.)
      (b) The Medo-Persian Empire (539-331 B.C.)
      (c) The Greek Empire (331-146 B.C.)
      (d) The Roman Empire (146 B.C. – A.D. 476)
    3. In pointing toward this last (fourth) empire, Daniel prophesied about the church: "And in the days of these kings the God of heaven will set up a kingdom which shall never be destroyed; and the kingdom shall not be left to other people; it shall break in pieces and consume all these kingdoms, and it shall stand forever" (Dan. 2:44).
    4. Here is a very clear and descriptive prophecy about the establishment of the church.
  B. The prophet _____ foretold the establishment of God's church.
    1. Isaiah wrote and spoke to a degenerate people who were turning away from God and who would soon find themselves away from God.
    2. But, Isaiah, the Messianic prophet, pointed to better and brighter days ahead for Israel and for all mankind.
    3. In pointing toward those better days, Isaiah prophesied about the church: "Now it shall come to pass in the latter days That the mountain of the Lord's house Shall be established on the top of the mountains, And shall be exalted above the hills; And all nations shall flow to it. Many people shall come and say, 'Come, and let us go up to the mountain of the Lord, To the house of the God of Jacob; He will teach us His ways, And we shall walk in His paths.' For out of Zion shall go forth the law, And the word of the Lord from Jerusalem" (Isa. 2:2-3).
    4. Here is a very clear and descriptive prophecy about the establishment of the church.

V. The Church of the Bible Was _____ of the New Testament.
  A. John the Baptist, the forerunner of Christ who was sent to prepare the way of the Lord, went about preaching, "Repent, for the kingdom of heaven is at hand!" (Matt. 3:2).
  B. When Jesus started His ministry, He went about preaching, "Repent, for the kingdom of heaven is at hand" (Matt. 4:17).
  C. When Jesus sent His twelve apostles out to the "lost sheep of the house of Israel," He told them to preach, "The kingdom of heaven is at hand" (Matt. 10:6-7).
  D. When Jesus sent seventy disciples out, He told them to preach, "The kingdom of God has come near to you" (Luke 10:9-11).
  E. The message being preached during the life and ministry of Jesus was preparing people for the imminent ("at hand") coming of the long-awaited church/kingdom.

VI. The Church of the Bible Was _____ Specifically and Clearly By _____.

A. The first time we ever read the word "church" in the Bible is in Matthew 16, and it is coming from the lips of Jesus. Isn't that fitting, that He spoke the word first?

    1. Peter made the great confession about the deity of Jesus (which was a revealed truth from heaven): "You are the Christ, the Son of the living God" (Matt. 16:16).

    2. Jesus then announced: "...On this rock _____, and the gates of Hades shall not prevail against it" (Matt. 16:18).

        (a) The church had not yet been established—it was still future.

        (b) The church would not be established by man—it would be built by Jesus.

        (c) The church would not find its origin or existence in man—it would be Jesus' church (notice the personal possessive pronoun "My").

        (d) The church would not be a temporary institution—nothing would overpower it.

    3. Jesus added that He would provide the "keys of the kingdom of heaven" (i.e., the means of entrance). Notice that He was using the terms "church" and "kingdom" interchangeably.

B. Just a short time later, after His promise in Matthew 16:18, Jesus made a promise to those living in His day.

    1. "Assuredly, I say to you that there are some standing here who will not taste death till they see the _____" (Mark 9:1).

    2. Jesus not only promised to build His church, He promised to build His church/kingdom in the lifetime of those hearing His words. It was not something thousands of years away; it was coming in that generation.

C. Cross-reference these promises of Jesus below and you'll see how He pinpointed the establishment of His church:

    1. That generation would "see the **kingdom** of God **present with power**" (Mark 9:1).

    2. Jesus promised the apostles: "Behold, I send the Promise of My Father upon you; but tarry in the city of **Jerusalem** until you are **endued with power from on high**" (Luke 24:49).

    3. Jesus promised the apostles: "But you shall receive **power when the Holy Spirit has come upon you**" (Acts 1:8).

    4. Summary of these verses: Kingdom Present → With Power → From on high → When Holy Spirit comes → On the apostles → In Jerusalem

VII. The Church of the Bible Was _____!

A. Christ did not merely make promises and set events on a course to ensure the establishment of the church. Christ took matters into His own hands to guarantee it.

B. The Bible makes a compelling statement about Jesus' personal investment in the church: "...He purchased [the church of God] _____" (Acts 20:28).

    1. The blood of Christ was necessary to "redeem" the lost from the power of Satan and sin (Eph. 1:7; 1 Pet. 1:18-19 + Rev. 7:14; 1 Cor. 6:19-20; Heb. 9:22).

    2. The blood of Christ continues to be necessary to "cleanse us from all" sin (1 Jn. 1:7,9).

C. The power of the blood of Jesus saves the individual from their sins (Rev. 1:5).

    1. Then, those who are saved are added together to body of the saved (Acts 2:47), which is the church "purchased with His own blood" (Acts 20:28).

    2. He loved the church so much that He "gave Himself for her" (Eph. 5:25).

D. No ordinary man could have established this church! Only deity could do that!

VIII. The Church of the Bible Was _____ on the Day of Pentecost _____.

    A. Acts chapter 2 describes the events that took place on the first Pentecost after the resurrection and ascension of Jesus. "When the Day of Pentecost had fully come" (2:1).

    B. Notice where the events of Acts 2 take place: Jerusalem (Acts 2:5).

    C. Notice upon whom the events at the beginning of Acts 2 befall: The apostles ("they" in 2:1 + "apostles" in 1:26).

    D. Notice who came in the events of Acts 2: "They were filled with the Holy Spirit" (2:4,17).

    E. Notice from where the Holy Spirit came in the events of Acts 2: "From heaven" (2:2).

    F. Notice what power was evident in the events of Acts 2: the apostles "began to speak with other tongues, as the Spirit gave them utterance" (2:4).

    G. Look at the arrows on the previous page that summarized Jesus' promises regarding His kingdom. Take what we just noticed about the events in Acts 2 and reverse the arrows. When you do that, what must have happened in Acts 2? What must have been established in Acts 2? What must have been "present" (cf. Mark 9:1) on that day?

    H. Summary of events in Acts 2: In Jerusalem → On the apostles → Holy Spirit comes → From on high → With Power → Kingdom Present

    I. The last verse of Acts 2 affirms the establishment of the church on that day: "And the Lord added to the church daily those who were being saved" (2:47, NKJV).

       1. Until this day, every statement about or in reference to the church/kingdom was always pointing forward to a future reality (incl. Mark 15:43; Luke 22:18, 29-30).

       2. Acts 2:47 is the first time that the church/kingdom is spoken of as a present reality.

    J. The events of Acts 2 are viewed in the Bible as "the beginning":

       1. Peter referred to that day and its events as "the beginning" (Acts 11:15).

       2. Jesus had foretold that the events of that day would be the "beginning" (Lk. 24:47).

       3. It was the beginning of the preaching of the gospel in its entirety (Acts 2:22-36).

       4. It was the beginning of the preaching of the gospel to "all nations" (Luke 24:47+Acts 1:5; cf. Matt. 28:19; Mark 16:15).

       5. It was the beginning of the preaching of God's plan of salvation and the remission of sins (Luke 24:47+Acts 2:38).

       6. It was the beginning of the new covenant in the Christian age (Heb. 8:7-13; 9:11-17; 10:15-18).

       7. It was the beginning of the church (Acts 2:40-47).

    K. After the events of Acts 2, every statement about or in reference to the church/kingdom was made about an institution that was already in existence.

       1. Before Acts 2, the church was always spoken of as yet in the future.

       2. After Acts 2, the church was always spoken of as being in existence.

          (a) "Great fear came upon all the church" (Acts 5:11).

          (b) "A great persecution arose against the church" (Acts 8:1).

          (c) "When they had appointed elders in every church" (Acts 14:23).

          (d) "He has...conveyed us into the kingdom" (Col. 1:13; cf. Heb. 12:28).

          (e) "I, John, both your brother and companion in the...kingdom" (Rev. 1:9).

IX. Conclusion

    A. The church of the Bible is NOT of human origin! It is of Divine origin! In reality, that is all I need to know. That is enough to recognize that it must have my utmost attention.

    B. The church was purposed, prophesied, prepared for, promised and purchased by God!

    C. The church was established in Acts 2, as an integral fulfillment of God's eternal plan.

    D. His church, which is still in existence today, must be an integral part of my eternal plan!

Lesson 4: The Distinct Nature of the Church

I. **The "Church" Is a Significant New Testament Doctrine.**
    A. The English word "church" is found over 100 times in the New Testament.
        1. The word's first occurrence is in Matthew 16:18.
        2. The word is not found in the Old Testament.
    B. Yet, the concept of the church is widely misunderstood today.
        1. People talk about "my church" or "your church" or "that church down the road."
        2. People often mistake the church for the material building or the physical location.
        3. People sometimes reduce the church to merely being some religious organization.
    C. To understand the true nature and significance of the church, we must study what the Bible says about it.

II. **The _____ of the Church Will Help in Understanding Its Nature.**
    A. "Church" comes from the Greek word *ekklesia*.
        1. *Ekklesia* is a compound Greek word: *ek* = out of, *kaleo* = to call.
        2. Thus, the church, by definition, is "the called out" or "the called out ones."
    B. The church is made up of ones who have been:
        1. ..."called out of darkness into His marvelous light" (1 Pet. 2:9).
        2. ...turned "from darkness to light, and from the power of Satan to God" (Acts 26:18).
        3. ..."delivered...from the power of darkness and conveyed...into the kingdom" (Col. 1:13).
    C. Those in the church have been "_____" by the gospel (2 Thess. 2:14).
        1. There is no other calling or other method by which one finds or enters the church than by the gospel.
        2. Of course, to be "called out," one must respond to the calling of the gospel. To ignore the calling of the gospel leaves one in darkness (and outside the church).

III. **The _____ of the Church (Specified in the N.T.) Will Help in Understanding Its Nature.**
    A. The church is composed of those who have been _____.
        1. "And the Lord added to the church daily those who were being saved" (Acts 2:47).
        2. People in the church are saved people, and saved people are in the church (Eph. 5:23).
    B. The church is composed of those who have been _____.
        1. "To the church of God which is at Corinth, to those who are sanctified in Christ Jesus, called to be saints" (1 Cor. 1:2).
        2. People in the church are sanctified (i.e., set apart) in and by Christ when they obey the gospel (1 Cor. 6:11), and the sanctified people are in the church.
        3. The identity of the person who has been "sanctified" is designated as a "saint." Saints are ones who have been set apart by God, and they make up the church.
    C. The church is composed of those who have been _____ to God.
        1. "...that He might reconcile them both to God in body through the cross" (Eph. 2:16).
        2. At one time, all of mankind has been "without Christ...having no hope" (Eph. 2:12).
        3. But, through the blood of Christ, He reconciled us back to God in His church.

IV. **The _____ Used for the Church in the N.T. Will Help in Understanding Its Nature.**
    A. The Bible uses various terms, depictions, images or figures to describe the church.
        1. The Lord's church is unlike anything else on this earth, therefore, the Lord utilized vivid pictures from daily living to help man understand and appreciate His church.
        2. By using words and concepts with which man is very familiar, God is able to convey the multifaceted nature of His church from a number of different angles.
        3. He also helps us to see how important His church is to Him.

B. The church is depicted in the New Testament as _____ – "the body of Christ" (1 Cor. 12:27).
  1. The spiritual body of the church is compared with the physical body of man.
     (a) As the physical body is composed of many parts, so is the spiritual body made up of many members (1 Cor. 12:14).
     (b) As the various parts of the physical body all work together harmoniously for the good of the whole body, so should the spiritual body function (1 Cor. 12:15-17).
     (c) While there are many parts to the body, there is just one body (1 Cor. 12:20).
     (d) While the various parts of the body are different and have different functions, each part is essential to the body—which is true of the physical body and the spiritual body (1 Cor. 12:21-25).
     (e) As the parts of the physical body care for each other, so should the members of the spiritual body, the church (1 Cor. 12:25-27).
  2. Christ "is the head of the body, the church" (Col. 1:18; cf. Eph. 1:22-23; 5:23). The terms "body" and "church" are used interchangeably/synonymously in the N.T.
  3. As there is one head, "there is one body" (Eph. 4:4).
  4. The emphasis of the body is upon the unity inherent within a body.
C. The church is depicted in the New Testament as _____ – "the household of God" (1 Tim. 3:15).
  1. "The household of God" is a depiction of the church as "the family of God."
     (a) In Acts 16:31-34, we read of the conversion of the jailer and "his household."
     (b) As "his household" was his family, "the household of God" is God's family.
  2. Those in God's family:
     (a) Have been "begotten" by Him (1 Pet. 1:3).
     (b) Are part of God's "whole family in heaven and earth" (Eph. 3:14-15).
     (c) Are God's "sons and daughters" (2 Cor. 6:18; cf. Gal. 3:26-27; 1 John 3:1-2).
     (d) Are "children of God...heirs of God and joint heirs with Christ" (Rom. 8:16-17).
     (e) Are brothers and sisters in Christ (1 Cor. 16:20; Acts 15:36; Jas. 2:15).
  3. God, as the one Father, has only one family, which should be united together in their bond and in their working together for the Father (Eph. 4:13-16).
  4. The emphasis of the family is upon the close-knit bond inherent within a family.
D. The church is depicted in the New Testament as _____ – "the kingdom of God" (Acts 1:3), "the kingdom of the Son of His love" (Col. 1:13), "the kingdom of heaven" (Matt. 3:2; 4:17; 10:7; 13:31; 18:3).
  1. Jesus identified the church as a kingdom, when He promised to build His church and then give the keys to the kingdom (Matt. 16:18-19), using the terms synonymously.
  2. Christ is the king of His kingdom (Rev. 19:16; 1:5), which is a spiritual or heavenly kingdom (John 18:36; Phil. 3:20).
  3. The kingdom is made up of people/citizens on this earth (who are "fellow citizens," Eph. 2:19), but its Ruler and its laws are from heaven (cf. Matt. 21:25)!
  4. The many parables that Jesus taught about "the kingdom of heaven" (see Matt. 13, et al) were intended to describe for us the nature of His church.
  5. The emphasis of the kingdom is upon the rule of law, government and obedient citizens inherent within a kingdom.

E. The church is depicted in the New Testament as _____ – *"to present you as a pure virgin to Christ" (2 Cor. 11:2).*
  1. The Bible likens the relationship between Christ and His church to the relationship between a husband and his wife/bride (Eph. 5:22-33).
     (a) "Christ...loved the church and gave Himself for her" (5:25).
     (b) The church is to be "a pure virgin" (2 Cor. 11:2), "not having spot or wrinkle or any such thing, but that she should be holy and without blemish" (Eph. 5:27).
     (c) The church is "married" to Christ (Rom. 7:4; cf. Rev. 22:17).
     (d) Christ is often called "the bridegroom" (Matt. 25:1-11; John 3:29).
  2. The emphasis of the bride is upon the intimate faithfulness inherent within a bride.
F. The church is depicted in the New Testament as _____ – *"the temple of God" (1 Cor. 3:16-17).*
  1. Individually, Christians are "the temple of the Holy Spirit" (1 Cor. 6:19-20), and collectively, the church as a whole is also "the temple of God" (1 Cor. 3:16-17).
  2. Peter describes this aspect of the church as being "a spiritual house," in which "a holy priesthood" (all Christians are priests) "offer up spiritual sacrifices acceptable to God" (1 Pet. 2:5; cf. Rev. 1:5-6; 5:10).
  3. The church is "a holy temple in the Lord" (Eph. 2:21), "built together for a dwelling place of God in the Spirit" (Eph. 2:22).
  4. The emphasis of the temple is upon the worship(ers) inherent within a temple.
G. The church is depicted in the New Testament as _____ – *"work today in my vineyard" (Matt. 21:28).*
  1. In His parables which depicted the nature of His kingdom, Jesus likened His kingdom to a vineyard and the members of His kingdom to laborers (Matt. 20:1-16; 21:28-44).
  2. Vineyards require hard labor, which is likely the imagery behind 1 Corinthians 15:58, "...be steadfast, immovable, always abounding in the work of the Lord, knowing that your labor is not in vain in the Lord."
  3. The emphasis of the vineyard is upon the hard work inherent within a vineyard.
H. The church is depicted in the New Testament as _____ – *"the flock of God" (1 Pet. 5:2).*
  1. In God's flock, Christians are the sheep and Jesus is "the Shepherd and Overseer of your souls" (1 Pet. 2:25; John 10).
  2. Sheep have a tendency to "stray" (Matt. 18:12-13; Isa. 53:6), which illustrates deeply the need for the "Good Shepherd" and following His voice (John 10).
  3. There is a tender relationship that exists between a shepherd and his sheep (Psa. 23).
  4. The emphasis of the flock is upon the following inherently necessary within a flock.
I. The church is depicted in the New Testament as _____ – *"endure hardship as a good soldier of Jesus Christ" (2 Tim. 2:3).*
  1. The church is engaged in a "war," but not a fleshly war with "carnal weapons" (2 Cor. 10:3-6), but against "spiritual hosts of wickedness" led by "the devil" (Eph. 6:11-12).
  2. Righteousness is always at constant odds with evil, and our "adversary the devil" would like nothing better than to destroy us (1 Pet. 5:8).
  3. As soldiers in the Lord's army (2 Tim. 2:3-4), we must "put on the whole armor of God" and stand in His strength for battle (Eph. 6:10-18).
  4. The emphasis on the army is upon defending against attacks and staying on target.

V. The _____ in Which the Word "Church" Is Used Will Help in Understanding Its Nature.

    A. The word "church" is used in a _____ sense in the New Testament.

        1. Jesus promised, "I will build my church" (Matt. 16:18).

        2. Jesus "purchased the church with His own blood" (Acts 20:28).

        3. Jesus "is head of the church" and "gave Himself" for the church (Eph. 5:23, 25).

        4. "The churches of Christ greet you" (Rom. 16:16).

        5. In verses like these, "church" is used in a universal, global, continual sense, to embrace all saved persons in the church from the first century until the end of time. Used in the plural simply represents all congregations of the church of Christ.

    B. The word "church" is used in a _____ sense in the New Testament.

        1. "In the church that was at Antioch" (Acts 13:1).

        2. "When they had appointed elders in every church" (Acts 14:23).

        3. "He sent to Ephesus and called for the elders of the church" (Acts 20:17).

        4. "Likewise greet the church that is in their house" (Rom. 16:5).

        5. "To the church of God which is at Corinth" (1 Cor. 1:2).

        6. In verses like these, "church" is used in a local sense of those Christians in a specific locality, community or city. The word "congregation" could often be understood.

    C. The word "church" or "churches" is used in a regional/provincial sense in the N.T.

        1. "The churches throughout all Judea, Galilee, and Samaria had peace" (Acts 9:31).

        2. "The churches of Asia greet you" (1 Cor. 16:19).

        3. "The grace of God bestowed on the churches of Macedonia" (2 Cor. 8:1).

        4. "To the churches of Galatia" (Gal. 1:2).

        5. "John, to the seven churches which are in Asia" (Rev. 1:4).

        6. In verses like these, "churches" is used regionally or provincially of multiple congregations within a given area, which are all part of the one church.

VI. Knowing the _____ of the Church Will Help in Understanding Its Essential Nature.

    A. The church is made up of the saved (Acts 2:47; cf. John 3:3-5), and only the saved will enter heaven (Rev. 21:27).

    B. Jesus is not only the "head of the church," "He is the Savior of the body" (Eph. 5:23).

    C. At the end of time, Jesus will "[deliver] the kingdom to God the Father" (1 Cor. 15:24).

    D. The following conclusions from these Bible truths are inescapable:

        1. The church/body/kingdom is made up of the saved, therefore, one must be in the church/body/kingdom in order to be saved.

        2. The eternal destiny of the church/body/kingdom is heaven, therefore, one must be in the church/body/kingdom to go to heaven.

    E. The eternal destiny of the church demands that it have an essential place in our lives today.

VII. Conclusion

    A. The church is God's called out people, who have obeyed the gospel in order to be saved.

    B. The Lord gives us so many angles from which to view His church. And from every vantage point, the Lord's description is of a beautiful, unique, essential institution.

    C. The Lord only has one place for His saved, sanctified, reconciled people—in His church!

    D. There is only one church! This is emphasized in the fact that the Lord has only:

        One body!   One family!   One kingdom!   One bride!

        One temple!   One vineyard!   One flock!   One army!

    E. I must be in His church to be saved and to go to heaven!

Lesson 5: The Unique Identity of the Church

I.   **There Is _____.**
   A. Understanding the unique identity of the church begins with understanding the singular nature of the church – there is only one.
      1. Jesus taught that there is only one church (Matt. 16:18).
         (a) Jesus promised to build His church, and He used the singular form of the word.
         (b) Jesus did not say anything about "churches" (plural) – only "church" (singular).
      2. Paul taught that there is only one church.
         (a) In 1 Corinthians 12, Paul taught that we are in "one body" (12:13, 20).
         (b) In Ephesians 4, Paul plainly stated, "There is one body" (4:4).
         (c) "The body" is the same as "the church" (Eph. 1:22-23; Col. 1:18), therefore, there is only one church.
   B. The _____ required by Christ for His church demands that there is only one church.
      1. All Christians are to be united in one body, which is the church of our Lord.
      2. Jesus prayed that Christians "all may be one, as You, Father, are in Me, and I in You; that they also may be one in Us" (John 17:20-21). That kind of unity can only be fulfilled in one church (not dozens, hundreds or thousands).
      3. The Holy Spirit begged Christians to "all speak the same thing, and that there be no divisions among you, but that you be perfectly joined together in the same mind and in the same judgment" (1 Cor. 1:10). That kind of unity demands one church.
   C. There is no such thing in the New Testament or in the mind of God as "joining the church of your choice."
      1. The Lord only has one church.
      2. The Lord adds those who are saved to His church (Acts 2:47).
      3. One must, therefore, search and identify the only church of the Lord's choice.
   D. _____ did not exist in the first century or in New Testament times.
      1. When the Lord established His church, there was only one church—His church.
      2. There were no denominations to "choose from" or to complicate the matter.
      3. The church of the New Testament is pre-denominational, existing centuries before man-made denominations ever came on the scene.
      4. All Christians were members of the same church—the one New Testament church.
      5. Today, people have grown so accustomed to viewing the church (or any church) as a denomination and thinking in denominational terms that it is very difficult to distance oneself from that mindset and think in purely New Testament terms.
         (a) However, such must be done in order to search for and identify the Lord's church.
         (b) Finding the church of the New Testament requires disconnecting our minds from man-made religious philosophy and connecting our minds to God's plan.
      6. When Jesus promised to build His church (Matt. 16:18) and when Jesus purchased the church with His own blood (Acts 20:28), He did not build, purchase, desire or intend for denominations. He built and purchased one church—His church.
   E. The goal of every serious Bible student must be to:
      1. Go back to the Bible and read and study about the church in the New Testament.
      2. With the identifying marks of the church from the New Testament, search for it diligently in the surrounding community and become a part of it.
      3. Restore the New Testament church (with all of its identifying marks from the New Testament) and be the church that Jesus loved and died for on the cross.

II. There Are Definite _____ of the One True Church in the New Testament.

   A. The only way to identify the one church of the New Testament today is to study the identifying marks of the church found in the New Testament. Here are just a few:

   B. **Identifying Mark: The church was _____.**
1. Jesus built the church of the New Testament (Matt. 16:18).
2. Jesus purchased the church of the New Testament (Acts 20:28).
3. Jesus is the head of the church of the New Testament (Eph. 5:23; 1:22-23; Col. 1:18).
4. Jesus is the lawgiver of the church of the New Testament (John 12:48; Acts 2:36).
5. If a "church" today has a different founder, it is not the one true church of the N.T.

   C. **Identifying Mark: The church was _____.**
1. Jesus is the foundation upon which the church was "laid" (1 Cor. 3:11).
2. Jesus is the chief cornerstone upon which the church was established (Eph. 2:20).
3. Jesus' deity is the rock upon which the church was built (Matt. 16:16-18).
4. If a "church" today has a different foundation, it is not the one true church of the N.T.

   D. **Identifying Mark: The church was _____.**
1. It was prophesied the church would be established in Jerusalem (Isa. 2:2-4; Zec. 1:16).
2. Jesus instructed His disciples to begin His work in Jerusalem (Luke 24:46-53).
3. The church came into existence in the city of Jerusalem in Acts 2 (2:1-5, 47).
4. If a "church" today was started in a different place, it is not the one true church.

   E. **Identifying Mark: The church was established on the first Pentecost after the resurrection of Christ (~ _____).**
1. It was prophesied that the church would be established in Roman days (Dan. 2:44).
2. It was prophesied that the church would be established in "the latter days" (Isa. 2:2).
    (a) Joel prophesied that the Spirit would be poured out in those days (Joel 2:28-32).
    (b) On the day of Pentecost (in Acts 2), Peter affirmed that the events taking place that day were "what was spoken by the prophet Joel" (Acts 2:16-21).
3. Jesus promised that the church would begin in His hearers' lifetime (Mark 9:1).
    (a) See Lesson 3 for a detailed analysis of the timing of the kingdom's establishment.
4. The church came into existence on the day of Pentecost in Acts 2 (2:1-4, 47).
5. If a "church" today was started at a different time, it is not the one true church.

   F. **Identifying Mark: The church _____ of its Founder, Owner and Savior.**
1. There are several designations for the church found in the New Testament:
    (a) "the church" (Eph. 3:10; Col. 1:18)
    (b) "the body of Christ" (Eph. 4:12; 1 Cor. 12:27)
    (c) "the church of God" (1 Cor. 1:2; 11:16; 15:9; 1 Tim. 3:5; 1 Thess. 2:14)
    (d) "the church of the living God" (1 Tim. 3:15)
    (e) "the church of the Lord" (Acts 20:28)
    (f) "church of the firstborn" (Heb. 12:23)
    (g) "churches of Christ" (Rom. 16:16)
    (h) "the kingdom of heaven" (Matt. 13:44; 16:19)
    (i) "the kingdom of God" (Mark 1:4; 9:1; Luke 10:9; Acts 1:3; 8:12)
    (j) "the kingdom of the Son of His love" (Col. 1:13)
    (k) "the house of God" (1 Tim. 3:15; Eph. 2:19)
    (l) These Scriptural expressions and designations are not "proper names" but marks of ownership. The church BELONGS to Christ, not any man or men.
    (m) If a "church" today wears a different name than one found in the N.T. (i.e., wears a man-made name), it is not the one true church of the New Testament.

2. There are several designations for the members of the church found in the N.T.:
   (a) "believers" (Acts 5:14; 1 Tim. 4:12)
   (b) "disciples" (Acts 6:1; 11:26; 19:30; 20:7)
   (c) "saints" (Rom. 1:7; 1 Cor. 1:2; Acts 9:13; Phil. 1:1)
   (d) "members" (1 Cor. 12:27; Eph. 2:19; 4:25)
   (e) "sons of God" (1 John 3:1-2; Gal. 3:26; Rom. 8:14-17)
   (f) "brethren" (1 Cor. 15:6; Jas. 1:2; 2 Pet. 1:10)
   (g) "priests" (1 Pet. 2:9; Rev. 1:6; 5:10)
   (h) "Christians" (Acts 11:26; 26:28; 1 Pet. 4:16)
   (i) If a "church" has members that wear different names than one found in the N.T., it is not the one true church of the New Testament.
3. There is definitely something in a name – especially when that name is Christ!

G. **Identifying Mark: The church follows only _____, doctrine, creed, discipline.**
   1. Man-made religions follow man-made doctrines from man-made creeds. Thus, the religions vary because the doctrines vary because the creeds vary.
   2. The one true church of the New Testament has only one law system, only one doctrine and only one creed that it follows – the New Testament (2 Tim. 3:16-17)!
   3. Since Christ is the head of the church (Eph. 5:23), and since He is Lord (Acts 2:36), and since His word is the all-authoritative standard of judgment (John 12:48), it follows that His word alone governs the teaching and practice of His church.
      (a) The Bible is verbally inspired (2 Tim. 3:16-17; 2 Pet. 1:20-21; 1 Cor. 2:9-13), inerrant (Psa. 19:7; Jas. 1:25; 1 Pet. 1:22-25) and all-sufficient (2 Pet. 1:3; Jude 3).
      (b) The Bible is not to be added to, taken from or modified in any way (Gal. 1:6-9; Rev. 22:18-19; 2 John 9-11).
      (c) The Bible alone makes us complete and thoroughly equips us for every good work (2 Tim. 3:17).
   4. Therefore, the one true church will "hear" Christ and only Him (Matt. 17:5).
      (a) The one true church will "continue steadfastly in the apostles' doctrine (Ac. 2:42).
      (b) The one true church will only "speak as the oracles of God" (1 Pet. 4:11).
      (c) The one true church will do all and say all by the authority of Christ (Col. 3:17).
   5. Church manuals, creeds and disciplines are a direct violation of Scripture.
      (a) If a church creed teaches more than the N.T., then it teaches too much.
      (b) If a church creed teaches less than the N.T., then it teaches too little.
      (c) If a church creed teaches different from the N.T., then it teaches error.
      (d) If a church creed teaches the same as the N.T., then it is not needed. We have the Bible!
   6. If a "church" today uses or follows any law system, doctrine, creed or discipline other than the New Testament, it is not the one true church.

H. **Identifying Mark: The church is _____ according to Scriptural guidelines.**
   1. The church has only one head – Christ (Eph. 1:22-23; 5:23; Col. 1:18), not a man.
   2. The church has no earthly headquarters, but only the one in heaven (1 Pet. 3:22).
   3. Congregations of the church are autonomous (Acts 14:23; 20:28).
   4. Congregations are to be overseen by a plurality of elders (Acts 14:23; 1 Pet. 5:2).
   5. Congregations are to have special servants called deacons (1 Tim. 3:8-13; Phil. 1:1).
   6. Congregations are to have evangelists to preach the gospel (2 Tim. 4:2-5; Eph. 4:11).
   7. An entire lesson will focus on this identifying mark later in this series.
   8. If a "church" today has a different organizational structure, it is not the true church.

I. **Identifying Mark: The church _____ as authorized by the New Testament.**
   1. The church follows a standard of worship—God's standard, not man's (John 4:23-24).
   2. The church worships on the first day of the week (Acts 20:7; 1 Cor. 11:20; 16:1-2).
   3. The church worships through partaking of the Lord's Supper (Acts 20:7; 1 Cor. 11:17-34).
   4. The church worships through prayer (Acts 2:42; 1 Cor. 14:15; 1 Thess. 5:17).
   5. The church worships through congregational singing (Eph. 5:19; Col. 3:16; Heb. 13:15).
   6. The church worships through giving as personally prospered (1 Cor. 16:1-2; 2 Cor. 8-9).
   7. The church worships through preaching of the gospel (Acts 2:42; 20:7; 2 Tim. 4:2).
   8. An entire lesson will focus on this identifying mark later in this series.
   9. If a "church" today worships in ways not authorized in the N.T., it is not the true church.
J. **Identifying Mark: The church has clear, universal and Scriptural _____.**
   1. One enters the church today in the very same way one entered the church in the N.T.
   2. Believers (Acts 16:31) who repent (Acts 2:38) and confess their faith (Rom. 10:9-10) are baptized into Christ (Gal. 3:27) to obtain the forgiveness of sins (Acts 2:38; 22:16).
   3. These are God's terms of entrance for all people of every nation (Acts 10:34-35; 8:12).
   4. Immersion into water is the culminating step that places one:
      (a) Into Christ (Gal. 3:27; Rom. 6:3).
      (b) Into the church of Christ (Acts 2:41-47).
      (c) Into the body of Christ (1 Cor. 12:13).
      (d) Into the family of God (Gal. 3:26-27).
      (e) Into the kingdom of God (John 3:3-5).
   5. Salvation is found only in Christ, in His church, in His body, in His family, in His kingdom (2 Tim. 2:10; Acts 2:47). One cannot be saved outside of Christ.
      (a) At the end of time, Jesus will deliver those in His kingdom/church/body to the Father in heaven (1 Cor. 15:24; Eph. 5:23-27).
      (b) "The gift of God is eternal life" (Rom. 6:23)! Where? In Christ! In His church!
   6. An entire lesson will focus on this identifying mark later in this series.
   7. If a "church" today teaches or practices different entrance terms, it is not the church.

III. **Conclusion**
   A. With thousands of man-made denominations in existence today, it can be challenging to:
      1. Identify the one true church.
      2. Think outside the denominational structure, terminology and mindset.
      3. Realize that denominations are not according to God's plan.
   B. The church that Jesus purchased and established in the New Testament still exists today.
      1. Daniel prophesied that it "shall never be destroyed...it shall stand forever" (2:44).
      2. Jesus promised that "the gates of Hades shall not prevail against it" (Matt. 16:18).
      3. The Hebrews' writer assured that it "cannot be shaken" (12:28).
      4. Once established (in Acts 2), it would (and will) always exist on this earth.
   C. Since the church still exists today, we must search for it and identify it.
      1. The only way to identify the N.T. church is to use its identifying marks in the N.T.
      2. If a "church" does not possess ALL of the identifying marks in this lesson (and others outlined in the N.T. but not included here), it is not the one true church of the New Testament.
      3. Do not settle for something that you think is "close." His true church still exists!
   D. The church is a divine institution with a unique identity—there is only one.
      1. The church is the most glorious institution on earth, because it belongs to Christ!
      2. As there is no salvation outside of His one church, let us obey His terms of entrance!

Lesson 6: The Organization of the Church

I. **The Church Is Spoken of in _____ in the New Testament.**

   A. See Roman numeral V in Lesson 4, "The Distinct Nature of the Church."

   B. The church is spoken of in a _____ sense in the New Testament (Matt. 16:18; Acts 20:28; Eph. 1:22-23; 5:23, 25; 1 Cor. 7:17; 11:16; 14:33; 2 Cor. 11:28; 1 Tim. 3:15).

      1. The universal sense embraces all saved persons of the earth from the first century until the end of time.

      2. The universal sense does not focus on any specific congregation of the Lord's people but on all of the Lord's people.

      3. The universal sense can appear in the singular "church" (Matt. 16:18) and the plural "churches" (1 Cor. 7:17), but all still referencing the "one body" (Eph. 4:4).

   C. The church is spoken of in a _____ sense in the New Testament (Acts 8:1; 13:1; 14:23; 20:17; Rom. 16:5; 1 Cor. 1:2).

      1. The local sense focuses on a congregation of the Lord's people in a specific locality, community or city.

      2. This is the sense in which the bulk of this lesson will focus.

   D. The church is spoken of in a regional/provincial sense in the New Testament (Acts 9:31; 1 Cor. 16:19; 2 Cor. 8:1; Gal. 1:2; Rev. 1:4).

      1. The regional/provincial sense embraces multiple congregations within a given area.

      2. Each of these congregations is separate from the others in the region (see IV below).

      3. Yet, each of these congregations is part of the one, global, universal church.

II. **Christ Is _____ of the Church.**

   A. This point cannot be overemphasized.

   B. The church is not a democracy. It is a theocracy, with Christ as King (Rev. 17:14).

   C. There is only one who has a right to rule or dictate in the church, and that is the One who has "all authority" (Matt. 28:18; Eph. 1:22-23; Acts 2:36).

      1. There is no earthly head of the church!

      2. The following find no mention, no place, and, therefore, no authority in the church: the Pope, Presiding Bishop, Right Reverend, Archdeacon, Cardinal, President, etc. Nor do ecclesiastical conventions, synods, councils, etc.

   D. In its universal sense, the church has _____.

      1. The New Testament has not authorized any church government beyond the local congregation (see III and IV below).

      2. Therefore, the New Testament does not authorize:

        (a) Any earthly headquarters for the church.

        (b) Any earthly organization/government of (or over) the church.

      3. The headquarters of the church is where the Head resides.

        (a) The church's Head resides in heaven (1 Pet. 3:22; Eph. 1:20-21).

        (b) The church must adhere to the orders given from heaven.

   E. Christ alone has authority (and all authority) over the universal church.

      1. His word and His truth are universal and must be universally taught, universally required and universally followed.

      2. There is no room at the universal level, regional level or local level for any modification of divine law. This point, also, cannot be overemphasized.

III. Each Local Church/Congregation Is to Be _____.

   A. At the local level, the church is to be organized according to the New Testament pattern.

   B. The "order" (i.e., organization structure) that God commanded at the local level of His church was to "appoint elders in _____ city" (Tit. 1:5).

     1. Paul followed this pattern when he "appointed elders in every church" (Acts 14:23).

     2. These men served as the local overseers of the local congregation under the rule and authority of Christ over His church.

   C. The divine "order" gives very specific qualifications that a man must meet in order to be considered for appointment as an elder.

     1. Read these qualifications in 1 Timothy 3:1-7, 11 and Titus 1:5-9.

   D. The divine "order" for the local congregation was a _____ of elders in each church.

     1. Note the plural "elder<u>s</u>" in Acts 14:23, 20:17, Philippians 1:1, Titus 1:5 & 1 Peter 5:1.

     2. The plural emphasizes that no one man can exercise oversight over a congregation. There must be more than one elder in each congregation.

     3. Therefore, there is no authority in the New Testament for a "pastor" to rule and govern over a congregation. A "preacher" is not, by definition, a "pastor." (See VI.)

   E. The divine "order" also _____ an eldership's oversight to _____ local congregation.

     1. Note the word "among" in Acts 20:28 and 1 Peter 5:1-2.

     2. The eldership's responsibility is limited to the church "among" which the elders lead (Acts 20:28; 1 Pet. 5:1-2).

     3. Just as one congregation must have a plurality of elders, those elders may only oversee the affairs of that one congregation and no other. (See IV.)

   F. Elders are designated by three Greek words, usually translated into six English words.

     1. The Greek *presbuteros* is translated into "presbyter" and "elder."
       (a) This word signifies an older man who has experience and wisdom.

     2. The Greek *episkopos* is translated into "overseer" and "bishop."
       (a) This word emphasizes the responsibility of oversight, superintendency and rule.

     3. The Greek *poimein* is translated into "shepherd" and "pastor."
       (a) This word emphasizes the work of caring, feeding and protecting the church.

     4. These three Greek words are used together in two passages about elders.
       (a) Acts 20:17, 28 – "[Paul] he sent to Ephesus and called for the <u>elders</u> *(presbuteros)* of the church. And when they had come to him, he said to them, "...Therefore take heed to yourselves and to all the flock, among which the Holy Spirit has made you <u>overseers</u> *(episkopos)*, to <u>shepherd</u> *(poimein)* the church of God which He purchased with His own blood."
       (b) 1 Peter 5:1-2 – "The <u>elders</u> *(presbuteros)* who are among you I exhort...<u>Shepherd</u> *(poimaino)* the flock of God which is among you, serving as <u>overseers</u> *(episkopos)*..."

     5. Summary: B-E-P-O-P-S: Bishops, Elders, Presbyters, Overseers, Pastors, Shepherds.

   G. The duty and work of elders is summarized in these designations for them.

     1. The primary work of elders is to tend to, care for, feed and protect the church.
       (a) This is emphasized in Acts 20:28-30, 1 Peter 5:1-3, 1 Timothy 3:1-7 & Titus 1:5-9.
       (b) The utmost importance of guiding the church to heaven is stressed in Hebrews 13:17—"they watch out for your souls, as those who must give account."

     2. Also underscored in the verses above is the elders' responsibility to "take care of the church" that is "entrusted" to them through proper oversight and example.

     3. Elders do not have authority to create new "laws," eliminate "laws" or modify divine laws. They only have authority to administer and require adherence to God's law.

IV. Each Local Church/Congregation Is _____.

A. "Autonomy" is a compound word, combining "auto"=self and "nomos"=law/rule. Thus, the word itself has the meaning of "_____."

   1. English dictionaries define autonomy as "the quality or state of being self-governing; the right of self-government; the state of existing or acting separately from others; an independent state or body."

B. Don't misunderstand or misapply the autonomy of the local congregation. A local congregation's autonomy does not negate or contradict the universal rule of Christ.

   1. A local congregation has no authority to decide on what day to worship. The rule of Christ has already decided and dictated that for all congregations of the church.

   2. A local congregation has no authority to decide the qualifications of its leaders. The rule of Christ has already decided and dictated that for all congregations of the church.

   3. Therefore, every local congregation is subject to the same universal law – the N.T., which must be taught (1 Cor. 4:17; 7:17) and obeyed the same (1 Cor. 1:10; Rom. 6:17).

C. Each local congregation of the Lord's church is autonomous (i.e., self-governing) in that:

   1. They are independent of and not subject to any other congregation or ecclesiastical organization/government.

   2. There is no authority of individual or body outside or above the local congregation.

   3. No man or body from outside a congregation may exercise rule or authority over that congregation.

   4. Each congregation is to independently judge matters of expediency, manage its own affairs, carry out its own work and deal with various circumstances that arise in accordance with the revealed will of Christ recorded in His all-authoritative Word.

D. Overseers of each congregation are permitted oversight only over the single congregation of which they are "_____" (Acts 20:28; 1 Pet. 5:1-2). (See III, E.)

   1. Individual overseers may not exercise authority outside their congregation, but only "over those entrusted" to them (1 Pet. 5:3).

   2. No congregation can be overseen or directed by someone not "among" them.

E. Each congregation of the Lord's church is its _____ separate body with its _____ leadership to govern _____ within (or "among") that body.

F. Individual local congregations are authorized in the New Testament to cooperate with each other in various effort or endeavors.

   1. This is seen in efforts of evangelism (Acts 11:19-30; Phil. 4:15-16).

   2. This is seen in efforts of edification (Acts 15:1-29; 18:27).

   3. This is seen in efforts of benevolence (Acts 11:27-30; Rom. 15:26-27; 1 Cor. 16:1-2).

   4. However, each congregation must continue to maintain its autonomy, and no authority may be exercised by one man or congregation over another congregation.

G. The first major departure from N.T. Christianity came in the organization of the church.

   1. Men were not satisfied with (1) the plurality of elders required, (2) the limited "rule" of elders over only one congregation, or (3) the autonomy of each congregation.

   2. Men began to create a hierarchal structure which: elevated one of the elders above the rest as "bishop"; positioned the "bishop" over multiple congregations in that region; appointed "archbishops" over multiple regions; and finally assigned one man as the supreme bishop over all the church.

   3. This deviation from God's pattern for the organization of the church led to a major departure (cf. Acts 20:28-31; 1 Tim. 4:1-3) and gave birth to Roman Catholicism.

   4. The church today must go back to the original organizational pattern for the church!

V. Each Local Church/Congregation Is to Have _____.

   A. While all Christians are servants, deacons are special servants with specified duties.

   B. The Greek word for "deacon" is *diakonos* (Phil. 1:1).

      1. The Greek word means "one who executes the commands of another...a servant, attendant, minister" *(Thayer's Greek Lexicon)*.

      2. The Greek word is translated: deacon, servant, minister.

      3. Thus, we understand that deacons are specialized servants in the church.

   C. Scripture gives very specific qualifications that a man must meet in order to be considered for appointment as a deacon. Read these qualifications in 1 Timothy 3:8-13.

   D. Insight can be gained into the work of deacons from Acts 6:1-7.

      1. While these men are not called "deacons," they appear to be functioning as such.

      2. There was a work (or "business," v. 3) that needed to be done.

         (a) The nature of this work was to "serve tables" or "deacon tables." A special task.

         (b) Just as in 1 Timothy 3:8-13, these men were to be "qualified for the job" (v. 3).

      3. The deacons were not "underlings"; they were appointed "over this business" (v. 3).

   E. In the church, there are important roles to be filled for the work of the church to thrive.

      1. In Acts 6, the apostles had work to do, and the "deacons" had assigned work to do.

      2. Today, the elders have work to do, and the deacons have assigned work to do.

      3. By definition, the work of deacons will be "service" oriented and assigned to them.

      4. When everyone fulfills their God-given roles, the church can grow (see Acts 6:7).

VI. Each Local Church/Congregation Needs to Have an _____.

   A. While all Christians are to preach the gospel to the lost, the church needs evangelists.

   B. The Greek words used for these men emphasize their role.

      1. Evangelists are to be "heralds"—proclaiming the message of the King (1 Tim. 2:7).

      2. Evangelists are to be "gospelizers"—spreading the good news of Jesus (2 Tim. 4:5).

      3. Evangelists have been charged with a heavenly message, which they must convey faithfully and completely, without modification. "Preach the word" (2 Tim. 4:2).

   C. In preaching, evangelists are to: "teach/instruct" + "convince/convict" + "rebuke/warn" + "exhort/plead" + "edify/encourage" + "comfort/console" (2 Tim. 4:2; 1 Cor. 14:3).

   D. An evangelist has the Scriptural responsibility to:

      1. Proclaim the pure gospel and thereby win souls to Christ (2 Tim. 4:2-5).

      2. Edify and build up the local congregation (Eph. 4:11-16; 1 & 2 Timothy and Titus).

      3. Protect the church and defend the faith (1 Tim. 1:3; 4:1-6; 6:20-21; 2 Tim. 4:1-5).

      4. Appoint and maintain qualified leadership in the local congregation (Tit. 1:5; 1 Tim. 3).

      5. Prepare and train other men to be preachers and teachers (2 Tim. 2:2).

   E. The preacher/evangelist is not the "_____" or the "_____."

      1. The elders (plurality) are the pastors, shepherds and overseers of the church.

      2. The preacher (just like every member, every deacon and every elder) is one of the members (sheep) of the congregation and is subject to the eldership.

      3. The preacher is not on a level "above" anyone else or to be "revered" as such.

VII. Conclusion

   A. There is only ONE head of the church and that is Christ – not any man or woman.

   B. The Lord's church must be organized and appoint leadership as instructed by the Lord.

   C. There is no Scriptural authority for modern forms of church government among the denominations, which do not follow the plurality of elders among a single congregation.

   D. The New Testament church will be organized according to the pattern in the New Testament. Any deviation from that pattern creates a man-made organization.

Lesson 7: The Mission and Work of the Church

I. **The Church of Christ Has a Glorious _____!**
   A. The church is made up of those who have been saved from their sins by Christ Jesus.
   B. All the saved have been banded together in one body, with a unified purpose.
   C. The ultimate and glorious purpose of the church is to _____, its Creator & Savior!
      1. "...to Him be glory in the church by Christ Jesus to all generations, forever and ever. Amen" (Eph. 3:20-21; cf. Rom. 11:36; Heb. 13:21).
   D. The church has no other and no greater purpose than giving (and being) glory to God!
      1. If a church aims for or finds itself serving some other purpose, it is not God's church!
      2. As the church "of Christ," the church seeks to be like Christ and to be able to say to the Father, as Christ did, "I have glorified You on the earth. I have finished the work which You have given Me to do" (John 17:4).

II. **The Church of Christ Has a Glorious _____!**
   A. As the church "of Christ," the church bears the same mission as Christ did.
   B. Christ and His church are inseparably connected – He is the head, the church is the body (Eph. 1:22-23; 5:23). Therefore, whatever mission He had is the mission that we have!
   C. The mission of Christ on earth was stated plainly, "For the Son of Man has come to seek and to save that which was lost" (Luke 19:10).
   D. The mission of the church is _____!
      1. Everything, E-V-E-R-Y-T-H-I-N-G that the church does must be to save souls!
      2. Every program in which the church engages must be directed to save souls!
      3. Every decision made by the leadership must be directed to save souls!
   E. In order to fulfill its purpose of glorifying God, the church must fulfill Christ's mission!

III. **The Church of Christ Has a Glorious _____!**
   A. In glorifying God and saving souls, the church also bears a responsibility to God's truth.
   B. Paul wrote the following to Timothy:
      "I write so that you may know how you ought to conduct yourself in the house of God, which is the church of the living God, the pillar and ground of the truth" (1 Tim. 3:15).
   C. Calling the church "the pillar and ground of the truth" is powerful:
      1. Note the definite article "the" before truth. The church is not just the pillar and ground of "a" truth, but of "the truth." Pure, objective, absolute, singular truth (cf. John 8:32)!
      2. In reality, the truth of God is its own pillar and ground, but in its mission to save souls, the church must support, maintain, stabilize, represent and defend the truth of God before all men.
      3. If the church does not faithfully stand as the pillar and ground of the truth among the various times and cultures of the world, who will?

IV. **The Church of Christ Has a Glorious _____!**
   A. The church has work to do! We are not merely saved to be saved! We are saved to _____!
   B. There are several things that make the church's work a glorious work:
      1. It is the work of the Lord (1 Cor. 15:58).
      2. It is work that we can and must do together (Phil. 1:27).
      3. The Lord equips us to do His work (Heb. 13:21).
      4. The Lord works <u>with</u> us as we work for Him (1 Cor. 3:5-9).
      5. The Lord works <u>in</u> us as we work for Him (Phil. 2:12-13; Heb. 13:21).
   C. God wanted His people to be happy, so He gave them something to do for Him!

V. In Its Mission of Saving Souls, the Church of Christ Is Given the Work of _____.

    A. "Evangelism" comes from the same root word as the word "gospel."

        1. "Gospel" means "good news," and "evangelism" means "bringing good news."

        2. So, evangelism involves preaching, announcing, making known good news.

        3. There is good news about sin:

            (a) "All have sinned and fall short of the glory of God" (Rom. 3:23).

            (b) "The wages of sin is death" (Rom. 6:23).

            (c) However, the good news or "gospel of Christ" is the "power of God unto salvation" from sin (Rom. 1:16).

    B. The church has been commissioned by Christ Himself.

        1. "And Jesus came and spoke to them, saying, 'All authority has been given to Me in heaven and on earth. Go therefore and make disciples of all the nations, baptizing them in the name of the Father and of the Son and of the Holy Spirit, teaching them to observe all things that I have commanded you; and lo, I am with you always, even to the end of the age.' Amen" (Matt. 28:18-20).

        2. "And He said to them, 'Go into all the world and preach the gospel to every creature. He who believes and is baptized will be saved; but he who does not believe will be condemned'" (Mark 16:15-16).

    C. In evangelism, the church is to _____.

        1. The good news of the manifold wisdom of God (Eph. 3:10-11).

        2. The good news about the death, burial and resurrection of Christ (1 Cor. 15:1-4).

        3. The good news of the saving power of the blood of Jesus (Matt. 26:28; Rev. 1:5).

        4. The good news of the abundant grace of God (1 Tim. 1:12-15; Tit. 2:11).

        5. The good news of forgiveness and freedom from sin (Acts 2:38; 22:16; Rom. 6:6-7).

        6. The good news of justification by faith in Christ (Rom. 3:21-26; 5:1-2; 1 Cor. 6:11).

        7. The good news of an eternal home promised in heaven (2 Cor. 5:1-8; John 14:1-3).

        8. "Go into all the world and <u>preach the gospel</u>..." (Mark 16:15).

    D. In evangelism, the church is to spread the good news _____.

        1. To our family members (John 1:39-42; Acts 16:31-34).

        2. To our friends (John 1:43-51; Acts 10:24-33).

        3. To our neighbors (Acts 1:8; 5:42).

        4. To our enemies (Acts 8:4-13; 10:28)

        5. To complete strangers (Acts 13-28)

        6. To everyone lost in sin (Matt. 18:11; Acts 17:16-34)

        7. To lost souls in our immediate area (1 Cor. 9:11-14; Acts 11:26)

        8. To lost souls around the world (Acts 1:8; 8:4; Col. 1:23)

        9. "Go <u>into all the world</u> and preach the gospel <u>to every creature</u>" (Mark 16:15).

    E. The church in the New Testament followed the commission and set an example for us.

        1. "They spoke the word of God with boldness" (Acts 4:31).

        2. "Daily in the temple, and in every house, they did not cease teaching and preaching Jesus as the Christ" (Acts 5:42).

        3. They "went everywhere preaching the word" (Acts 8:4).

        4. They "turned the world upside down" (Acts 17:6).

        5. From them "the word of the Lord has sounded forth...in every place" (1 Thess. 1:8).

        6. Only thirty years after the establishment of the church in Acts 2, Paul was able to write, "the gospel...was preached to every creature under heaven" (Col. 1:23).

    F. The church's work in evangelism must be focused on saving souls.

VI. In Its Mission of Saving Souls, the Church of Christ Is Given the Work of _____.

A. "Edification" has to do with _____ (spiritual growth).

   1. When the work of evangelism is fruitful and individuals become Christians, the mission of saving souls (their souls) is not complete.

   2. Once they're saved, Christians need to be "rooted and built up in Him and established in the faith" (Col. 2:7).

   3. In the Great Commission, true disciples are made not only by baptizing them but by "teaching them to observe all things" (Matt. 28:20).

B. It is essential for every Christian to grow spiritually!

   1. Every Christian must "grow in the grace and knowledge of our Lord" (2 Pet. 3:18).

   2. Christians, who were not growing properly in the first century, were reprimanded for their stagnation and lack of spiritual growth (Heb. 5:12).

   3. Spiritual growth must take place with an increase in knowledge of sound doctrine and then must be exhibited with an increase in faithful Christian living (2 Pet. 1:5-9).

   4. Satan is ever-busy, seeking opportunities to prevent, stunt, divert and reverse spiritual growth in a Christian's life (Luke 8:12; Eph. 6:10-13); therefore, we must be ever vigilant and determined in our efforts (1 Pet. 5:8-9).

C. In edification, the church is responsible for _____.

   1. God has organized and structured His church, in order that (Eph. 4:12-15):

     (a) The saints can be <u>equipped</u> for the work of the ministry (v. 12).

     (b) The body can be <u>edified</u> and <u>built up</u> (v. 12).

     (c) The church can reach a unified level of <u>faith and knowledge</u> of Christ (v. 13).

     (d) The brethren may <u>not be carried</u> about by false doctrines and cunning (v. 14).

     (e) The body may <u>grow up</u> in all things into the head, Christ (v. 15).

     (f) The whole body might be <u>joined and knit</u> together (v. 16).

     (g) The body can be properly fed & engage in effective exercise (individually & collectively).

   2. When a local congregation is properly edifying the body, it will result in (Eph. 4:16):

     (a) Every member effectively working to do <u>his/her share</u> (v. 16).

     (b) Continual <u>growth</u> of the body and continued <u>edification</u> of itself (v. 16).

     (c) The building up of the individual member and the entire body.

   3. We must all "strive to excel in building up the church" (1 Cor. 14:12).

D. Collectively, the church is edified and edifies one another through a variety of means:

   1. Encouraging one another edifies the church (individually and collectively).

     (a) Barnabas, the Son of Encouragement, "...was glad, and encouraged them all that with purpose of heart they should continue with the Lord" (Acts 11:23).

     (b) "Exhort one another daily, while it is called 'Today'" (Heb. 3:13).

   2. Worshiping together edifies the church (individually and collectively).

     (a) In the context of worship, "Let all things be done for edification" (1 Cor. 14:26).

     (b) "And let us consider one another in order to stir up love and good works, not forsaking the assembling...but exhorting one another..." (Heb. 10:24-25).

   3. Studying the Bible together edifies the church (individually and collectively).

     (a) "...Desire the pure milk of the word, that you may grow thereby" (1 Pet. 2:2).

     (b) "...the word of His grace, which is able to build you up" (Acts 20:32).

   4. Engaging in fellowship together edifies the church (individually and collectively).

     (a) "I thank my God...for your fellowship in the gospel..." (Phil. 1:3-5).

     (b) "So they...entered the house...they encouraged [the brethren]" (Acts 16:40).

E. The church's work in edification must be focused on saving souls.

VII. In Its Mission of Saving Souls, the Church of Christ Is Given the Work of _____.

    A. "Benevolence" has to do with supplying _____ service and help to persons in need.

        1. Note that benevolence is dealing with physical and material needs (not spiritual).

        2. Note that benevolence is supplying only temporary assistance (not permanent).

        3. However, the ultimate goal of all benevolence must be on the eternal.

    B. Helping and serving those in need is a command (and an expectation) of God!

        1. "Let him who stole steal no longer, but rather let him labor, working with his hands what is good, that he may have something to give him who has need" (Eph. 4:28).

        2. "Therefore, as we have opportunity, let us do good to all, especially to those who are of the household of faith" (Gal. 6:10; cf. 1 Tim. 5:16).

        3. "Pure and undefiled religion before God and the Father is this: to visit orphans and widows in their trouble, and to keep oneself unspotted from the world" (Jas. 1:27).

    C. Helping and serving those in need emulates and serves Christ Himself!

        1. "...The Son of Man did not come to be served, but to serve" (Matt. 20:28).

        2. "Assuredly, I say to you, inasmuch as you did it to one of the least of these My brethren, you did it to Me" (Matt. 25:34-40; cf. 25:41-45).

    D. Helping and serving those in need is to be done by the church (not just individuals)!

        1. The church must be characterized by a generous spirit and a compassionate heart!

        2. The church in Antioch "determined to send relief to the brethren dwelling in Judea. This they also did, and sent it..." (Acts 11:27-30).

        3. The churches in Macedonia and Achaia were pleased "to make a certain contribution for the poor among the saints who are in Jerusalem" (Rom. 15:25-27).

    E. Helping and serving those in need must focus on souls and getting them to heaven!

        1. The church is not set up as a charitable organization engaged in social betterment!

        2. The church is not set up to minister merely to physical and temporal needs!

        3. The church IS set up to seek and save the lost with the gospel of Christ (Rom. 1:16)!

    F. The church's work in benevolence must be focused on saving souls.

VIII. Conclusion

    A. The purpose and work of the church is NOT to:

        1. Operate in the political arena or shape public policy.

        2. Operate as a community center or social welfare organization.

        3. Take the place of the home or the parents in the lives of children.

        4. Furnish entertainment or be a recreation center.

        5. Make deposits in the bank and keep a large balance of funds.

        6. Focus on the material or non-spiritual needs of members or non-members.

    B. The purpose and work of the church IS to:

        1. Glorify God and manifest His wisdom.

        2. Fulfill Christ's mission to save souls.

        3. Stand firm as the pillar and ground of the truth.

        4. Labor for God and with God in carrying out His work on this earth through:

            (a) Evangelism, spreading the good news of Christ and salvation through Him.

            (b) Edification, building up the brethren to faithful lives of service to Him.

            (c) Benevolence, assisting those in need with material and temporary help.

        5. Focus on souls and leading them to heaven.

    C. The mission and work of the church is great and glorious because the God we serve is Himself great and glorious!

Lesson 8: Worship of the Church on the Lord's Day

I. God Created Man with an Instinctive Need to Worship.
   A. Created in God's image, man is innately designed to seek Him (Acts 17:26-27).
   B. Sometimes, when there is no proper instruction, this instinct will lead to worshiping the wrong image (Ex. 32:8; 2 Kgs. 21:3; Dan. 3:7; Acts 10:25; 14:12-18; 17:16; Rev. 22:8).
   C. By following proper instruction, there is something intensely thrilling and satisfying about worshiping God (Psa. 26:8; 27:4-6; 42:1-2; 122:1).
   D. The first recorded activity of man outside the Garden of Eden was worship (Gen. 4:3-5).

II. God Has Always Provided Mankind with Instruction Regarding _____.
   A. The first record of worship in the Bible shows there is acceptable & unacceptable worship.
      1. God "respected Abel and his offering, but He did not respect Cain and his..." (Gen. 4:4-5).
      2. Right away Bible readers learn that not all worship is alike, nor is all worship accepted.
      3. The Bible later reveals that Abel offered his worship "by faith," for he heard and followed the Word of God on the matter (Heb. 11:4 + Rom. 10:17).
      4. Thus, we can know that God provided Cain & Abel with instruction regarding worship.
   B. God continued to provide instruction through the Mosaic and Christian Dispensations.
      1. The books of Exodus and Leviticus gave details for acceptable Jewish worship.
      2. The books of the New Testament give details for acceptable Christian worship.
      3. God has always explained the purpose, means and benefits of acceptable worship.
   C. It is essential that worshipers understand and offer acceptable worship to God!

III. God Has Warned Christians About Worship That Is _____.
   A. Idol worship is not acceptable to God (1 Cor. 10:14).
      1. Idols can be stone/wooden objects (Ac. 17:23), money (Col. 3:5) or self (Phil. 2:21).
   B. _____ worship is not acceptable to God (Acts 17:23).
      1. To seek to worship God "without knowing" Him or understanding His will for worship is to worship in ignorance and unacceptably.
   C. _____ worship is not acceptable to God (Matt. 15:8-9).
      1. To seek to worship God merely externally (without the heart) or to worship based on the doctrines or commandments of men is to worship in vain and unacceptably.
   D. _____ worship is not acceptable to God (Col. 2:23).
      1. To seek to worship God according to "self-imposed religion, false humility" or according to one's own feelings, rules and devisings is to worship unacceptably.

IV. God Has Clearly Defined True and Acceptable Worship for Christians.
   A. The primary Greek word for "worship" is a compound word *proskuneo*.
      1. *Pros* means "towards" and *kuneo* means "to kiss"; literally, "to kiss towards."
      2. The word is defined, "to make obeisance, do reverence to; an act of homage."
      3. In worship, the worshiper acts to show reverence to the one being worshiped.
   B. Worship is a definite act that one performs, with a start and a finish to it (Matt. 2:2, 11).
   C. Worship is a definite act that requires one's _____ to accomplish it fully.
      1. Abraham told his servants, "The lad and I will go yonder and worship, and we will come back to you" (Gen. 22:5). A definite act, with a start and a finish to it.
      2. "So Abraham took the wood of the burnt offering...the fire...and a knife...And Abraham built an altar there and placed the wood in order...And Abraham stretched out his hand and took the knife" (Gen. 22:6-10). What Abraham had called "worship" (in his words to his servants) required his full participation to accomplish.
   D. Worship is a solemn, sacred and holy act! It requires man's utmost!

V. God Has Clearly Detailed the _____ for True and Acceptable Worship.

   A. "True worship" is an expression used by Jesus, not invented by man.

      1. "But the hour is coming, and now is, when the true worshipers will worship the Father in spirit and truth; for the Father is seeking such to worship Him. God is Spirit, and those who worship <u>Him</u> must worship in <u>spirit</u> and <u>truth</u>" (John 4:23-24).

      2. God is seeking "true worshipers," which implies there are "false worshipers" (see III).

      3. God is seeking "true worshipers" and has revealed how to be a "true worshiper."

      4. God has never left man to his own thoughts and devices in how to worship Him.

      5. The fact that God is seeking such distinctive worship means it must be identifiable.

   B. True worship must be <u>directed TOWARD the proper object</u> – _____.

      1. "You shall worship the Lord your God, and Him only you shall serve" (Matt. 4:10).

      2. "Worship God" (Rev. 22:9).

      3. Worship involves proper reverence and awe for God and for God alone (Heb. 12:28).

      4. True reverence for God will lead to worship from the heart according to His Word!

      5. God alone is the only worthy object or audience of worship!

   C. True worship must be <u>directed FROM the proper attitude</u> – _____.

      1. Worship must be directed from a heart filled with faith and love (John 14:15).

      2. Worship must be directed from a heart fully devoted to the Lord (Matt. 22:37-38).

      3. Worship must be directed from a heart of joy, gladness & thanksgiving (Psa. 118:24).

      4. Worship is not merely an outward act, but acceptable worship must start from deep within a man's heart (Matt. 15:7-9). Otherwise, it is vain hypocrisy.

   D. True worship must be <u>directed BY the proper standard</u> – _____.

      1. Worship done "in truth" is by the standard of God's Word (John 17:17).

      2. God alone has the authority to tell man what to do in worship to be acceptable.

      3. All things, including worship, must be done by the authority of Christ (Col. 3:17).

      4. All parts of worship must be measured by the standard of God's Word.

   E. True worship, to God in spirit and in truth, is a MUST.

      1. Note the word "must" in John 4:24. This is not optional. It is absolute.

      2. True worship "MUST" be BOTH from the heart and according to His Word to be true!

VI. God Has Authorized _____ for Worship in the New Testament Church.

   A. When the church was established in Acts 2, Scripture records for us that "they continued steadfastly in the apostles' doctrine and fellowship, in the breaking of bread, and in prayers...praising God and having favor with all the people" (Acts 2:42, 47).

      1. They worshiped thru five avenues: Preaching (apostles' doctrine), Giving (fellowship), Lord's Supper (the breaking of bread), Praying (prayers), Singing (praising God).

   B. God has authorized _____ as an avenue of worship.

      1. The church is to engage in a teaching & study of Scripture in worship (Acts 20:7).

      2. Preachers must handle aright the word (2 Tim. 2:15; 4:2), speak only the oracles of God (1 Pet. 4:11; Gal. 1:8-9) and teach "the whole counsel of God" (Acts 20:27).

      3. Worshipers/Listeners must desire the word (1 Pet. 2:2), demand the unadulterated truth (Gal. 1:8-9) and receive the message as the Bereans did (Acts 17:10-11).

   C. God has authorized _____ as an avenue of worship.

      1. Common "orders" were commanded to all churches for giving (1 Cor. 16:1).

      2. Giving is to be done according as one "may prosper" (1 Cor. 16:2).

      3. Giving is to be done as one "purposes in his heart" and "not grudgingly or of necessity," remembering that "God loves a cheerful giver" (2 Cor. 9:7).

      4. One's giving as worship is a freewill offering between a worshiper and his God.

5. God's blessings to us are in proportion to our giving to Him (2 Cor. 9:6; Luke 6:38).
6. The funds are to be used for reaching the lost, teaching the saved & helping the needy.
D. God has authorized the _____ as an avenue of worship.
   1. The Lord's Supper involves two elements, unleavened bread and fruit of the vine, as emblems of the Lord's body and His blood (Mark 14:22-25).
   2. Partaking of the elements is a memorial to Christ (1 Cor. 11:24-25) and the ultimate sacrifice that He made on the cross for our sins (Matt. 26:28; 1 Cor. 15:3; Isa. 53:4-8).
   3. By partaking of the Lord's Supper, we "proclaim His death" (1 Cor. 11:26).
   4. When partaking of the Lord's Supper, we must discern the Lord's body and examine ourselves (1 Cor. 11:27-29).
   5. Partaking of the Lord's Supper is to be done every Sunday (Acts 20:7; 1 Cor. 16:1-2).
   6. See Lesson 10 for more details on the Lord's Supper.
E. God has authorized _____ as an avenue of worship.
   1. The early church "continued steadfastly in...prayers" (Acts 2:42).
   2. Prayers in public worship must be sincere and understandable (1 Cor. 14:15).
   3. As with all avenues of worship, men are to take the lead in the prayer (1 Tim. 2:8).
   4. Collective prayer in worship acknowledges a mutual love and dependence on God.
F. God has authorized _____ as an avenue of worship.
   1. As with all avenues of worship, music in worship must be authorized by God.
   2. God has authorized the singing of psalms, hymns & spiritual songs (Eph. 5:19; Col. 3:16).
      (a) Singing in worship is intended firstly to praise God ("to the Lord").
      (b) Singing is also "to one another" as a form of "teaching and admonishing."
      (c) Everyone is engaged in the singing, and the heart is the melodious instrument.
   3. As with praying, our singing must be sincere and understandable (1 Cor. 14:15).
   4. See Lesson 10 for more details on music in worship.

VII. God Has NOT Authorized His Church to Worship on the _____.
A. There are some who contend that the church must worship on the Sabbath (Saturday).
   1. They argue that the Sabbath was part of the Ten Commandments and is still binding.
   2. They argue that the Sabbath is a perpetual (forever) ordinance to keep.
   3. They argue that Sabbath keeping goes all the way back to creation (before Judaism).
B. The teaching of the Bible regarding Sabbath observance is very clear.
   1. In Genesis 2:2-3, "the seventh day" is referenced three times, but not "the Sabbath."
      (a) "God" and "His work" are referenced three times, but man is not referenced at all.
      (b) There is nothing in this passage to teach that God expected anything of man.
   2. The Sabbath is not mentioned for the first 2,500 years of Bible history (65 chapters).
   3. The command to observe the Sabbath was part of the law that God made (Deut. 5:12):
      (a) With the Jews only ("Israel" + "with us" [3x], Deut. 5:1-3).
      (b) With the Jews at Mt. Sinai (Deut. 5:2; Ex. 19-20; Neh. 9:13-14).
      (c) But not before Mt. Sinai ("today") or "with our fathers" (Deut. 5:1-3; Neh. 9:13-14).
      (d) As a sign with Israel and no other nation(s) (Ex. 20:1-2; 31:12-17; Ezek. 20:12, 20).
      (e) To remember that they had been slaves in the land of Egypt (Deut. 5:15; Ex. 20:2).
   4. There is no command or example in the Bible of Sabbath observance by any non-Jew.
      (a) By noting its purpose, it would have been meaningless to any other people!
      (b) Observing the Sabbath was not a universal command.
C. The covenant/law that God made at Mt. Sinai included _____ (Ex. 34:27-28; Deut. 4:13; 9:9-11; 1 Kgs. 8:9, 21).
D. The covenant/law that God made at Mt. Sinai was abrogated by God Himself.

1. God foretold and fulfilled the making of a "new covenant" (Jer. 31:31-34; Heb. 8:6-13).
2. The covenant/law that was abrogated included the Ten Commandments:
   (a) "The law," to which we are "dead" and from which we "have been delivered," was the one that commanded, "You shall not covet" (Rom. 7:1-7).
   (b) The law, which included "sabbaths," was "wiped out...taken out of the way...nailed to the cross" (Col. 2:14-17).
   (c) The law, which was "written and engraved on stones," has "passed away," been "taken away" and no longer "remains" (2 Cor. 3:3-18).
E. The covenant (including the Ten Commandments) was only "forever" in the sense that it was not to cease within the timeframe for which it was intended.
   1. The same word "forever" used of the Sabbath (Ex. 12:14) was used of Pentecost (Lev. 23:21) and the Feast of Tabernacles (Lev. 23:41).
   2. The same word "perpetual" used of the Sabbath (Ex. 31:16-17) was used of burning incense (Ex. 30:8), burnt offerings (Ex. 29:42) and sin offerings (Ex. 30:10).
   3. None of these things are part of God's covenant with man today, because they were only to last "perpetually" for the years that the first covenant was in force.
F. Anyone seeking to be justified by the law of Mt. Sinai is "estranged from Christ" (Gal. 5:4).

VIII. God Has Authorized His Church to Worship on _____ (the First Day of the Week).

A. Under the new covenant, the Lord established a new religion, a new institution, new commandments, a new feast, and a new day to worship—"the Lord's Day" (Rev. 1:10).
B. The first day of the week has great significance to Christians because of what happened.
   1. It was the day that Jesus Christ was raised from the dead (Mark 16:9).
   2. It was the day that Jesus was declared "to be the Son of God with power" (Rom. 1:3-4).
   3. It was the day that Jesus gathered with His disciples after His resurrection (Jn. 20:19, 26).
   4. It was the day that the Holy Spirit came upon the apostles as promised (Acts 2:1-4).
      (a) The day of Pentecost was always on the first day of the week (Lev. 23:15-16).
   5. It was the day that the gospel was preached fully for the first time (Acts 2:14-40).
   6. It was the day that the church/kingdom was established with power (Acts 2:1, 41, 47).
   7. It was the day that the church assembled in New Testament times (Acts 20:7)
   8. It was the day that the church assembled to commune with the Lord (Acts 20:7).
   9. It was the day that the church assembled every week (1 Cor. 16:1-2; 4:17; 7:17).
C. The first day of the week has great significance to Christians because it does to the Lord!
   1. The Lord requires the "first" from us (Gen. 4:4; Prov. 3:9; Matt. 6:33).
   2. The Lord chose the "first" day of the week for Himself and His people.
      (a) The early church assembled every first day of the week (Acts 20:7; 1 Cor. 16:1-2).
      (b) The early church assembled to commune with the Lord (Acts 20:7; Mark 14:25).
      (c) Church historians record that early Christians always assembled on Sunday.
   3. Therefore, the Christian must make worship on the Lord's Day a priority (Heb. 10:25).

IX. Conclusion

A. What a sacred privilege given to Christians that we can worship the Almighty God!
B. What a blessing to be given specific instructions to ensure our worship is acceptable!
C. May our worship always be focused on God and truly glorify Him!
D. May our worship always be offered with the proper heart of utmost reverence!
E. May our worship always be according to God's authorized avenues specified in His Word!
F. May our worship never focus on the performance or entertainment of the worshiper!
G. May our worship edify (1 Cor. 14:26), without confusion (14:33), and be orderly (14:40)!
H. May the Lord's Day have the significance to us that it has to the Lord!

Lesson 9: The Lord's Supper

I. Jesus _____ on the Night Before His Crucifixion.

    A. The institution of the Lord's Supper is recorded in four passages—Matthew 26:26-29; Mark 14:22-25; Luke 22:17-20; 1 Corinthians 11:23-26.

    B. Jesus instituted the Lord's Supper after observing the Jewish Passover with His apostles.

        1. Passover commemorated God's deliverance of the Jews from Egyptian bondage.

        2. Specifically, the Passover reminded the Jews of the occasion when, because of the blood on their lintel and doorposts, the Lord did "pass over" their homes (Ex. 12:23).

        3. It was not by accident that Jesus instituted His supper at the Passover feast (cf. 1 Cor. 5:7).

    C. When instituting His feast, Jesus emphasized that it was "_____."

        1. "I will no longer drink of the fruit of the vine until that day when I drink it <u>new</u> in the kingdom of God" (Mark 14:25). What was "new"?

        2. The Lord's Supper was a "new" feast/memorial.

            (a) The Jews had observed and celebrated many feasts/memorials under their law, commemorating a number of events in Jewish history.

            (b) This feast/memorial being instituted by Jesus was a "new" feast/memorial, commemorating a "new" deliverance made possible by the blood of Christ.

        3. The Lord's Supper was in a "new" kingdom.

            (a) Jesus foretold of His partaking of the elements "in the kingdom," which was soon to be established (Mark 9:1).

            (b) This was the kingdom which was long awaited by the Jews, who followed Old Testament prophecies. The kingdom was/is the church (Matt. 16:18-19).

        4. The Lord's Supper was of a "new" covenant.

            (a) Jesus said, "This cup is the <u>new</u> covenant in My blood" (Luke 22:20).

            (b) The blood of Jesus would abolish the old covenant (Eph. 2:15; Col. 2:14) and usher in a new covenant (Heb. 9:15-17).

            (c) The blood of Jesus provided "remission of sins" (Matt. 26:28), in order for one to enter into the new covenant with the Lord (Heb. 9:18-10:4).

        5. The Lord's Supper was on a "new" day. (See Roman numerals VII & VIII in Lesson 8.)

            (a) On the last day of the week, Jews remembered their deliverance from bondage (Ex. 20:8-11).

            (b) On the first day of the week (the day on which Christ rose triumphant over death), Christians were to remember their deliverance from bondage.

        6. The Lord's Supper was "new" – a new feast, of a new memorial, in a new kingdom, by a new covenant, on a new day, for a new people.

II. Jesus Instituted the Lord's Supper to Be Extraordinarily _____.

    A. Jesus instituted the Lord's Supper as a time for _____ (1 Cor. 10:15-22).

        1. "Communion" is not just what it is called; "communion" is what is happening.

        2. "The cup of blessing which we bless, is it not the <u>communion</u> of the blood of Christ? The bread which we break, is it not the <u>communion</u> of the body of Christ?" (1 Cor. 10:16).

        3. The Greek word for "communion" is *koinonia,* which is the word for "fellowship, participation, partnership, sharing." This is what we enjoy when partaking.

        4. In the Lord's Supper (emphasize "Lord's"), we commune with Christ Himself.

            (a) He promised to "drink it new with you [or us] in My Father's kingdom" (Mt. 26:29).

            (b) Imagine partaking of the Lord's Supper with Jesus partaking next to you.

B. Jesus instituted the Lord's Supper as a time for _____ (1 Cor. 11:23-25).
    1. God knew that His people needed memorials, in order to remember Him.
        (a) When crossing the Jordan, the Israelites selected and set up twelve stones as a memorial of what God had done (Josh. 4:1-24).
        (b) Upon delivering the Israelites from bondage in Egypt, the Lord established the Passover feast as a memorial of what He had done (Ex. 12:1-28)
    2. Twice Jesus commanded, "Do this in remembrance of Me" (1 Cor. 11:24-25).
    3. The two elements of the Supper themselves provide the key to the memorial.
        (a) The unleavened bread was an emblem of His sinless, lifeless body: "This is My body which is given for you; do this in remembrance of Me" (Luke 22:19).
        (b) The fruit of the vine was an emblem of His shed blood: "This is My blood of the new covenant, which is shed for many" (Mark 14:24).
        (c) Scripture does not teach that the elements transform into the actual body and blood of Jesus when we partake. "Transubstantiation" is man-made doctrine.
    4. In the Lord's Supper, we are to be "discerning the Lord's body" (1 Cor. 11:29).
        (a) Our minds are to separate or discriminate our thoughts to His body on the cross.
        (b) Our hearts must remember that Christ suffered and died for us, shedding His blood, in order that we might be delivered from the slavery to sin.
C. Jesus instituted the Lord's Supper as a time for _____ (1 Cor. 11:27-30).
    1. "But let a man examine himself, and so let him eat of the bread and drink of the cup."
    2. While reflecting upon the sacrificial death of Christ, one must reflect on his own life.
        (a) We are not "examining others," to determine an "open" or "closed communion."
        (b) Each Christian is to examine the only life he can thoroughly examine—his own.
        (c) "How is the death of Christ affecting me? How is my life conforming to His death?"
D. Jesus instituted the Lord's Supper as a time for _____ (1 Cor. 11:26).
    1. "...as you eat this bread and drink this cup, you proclaim the Lord's death till He comes."
    2. The regular observance of the Lord's Supper is a regular message to the world that Jesus died for all and shed His blood that all might be saved.
    3. The regular observance of the Lord's Supper is also a regular message to the world that Jesus is coming again and all must be prepared when He comes.
E. Jesus instituted the Lord's Supper to be observed in a "_____" (1 Cor. 11:27, 29).
    1. This has nothing to do with the "worthiness" of the partaker to eat and drink.
        (a) The word is not an adjective to modify the partaker.
        (b) The word is an adverb to modify the verb, emphasizing the manner of partaking.
    2. There are two keys in the passage for partaking in a "worthy manner."
        (a) First, one must "remember" and "discern" the body and blood of the Lord.
        (b) Second, one must "examine himself" in light of the body and blood of the Lord.
    3. To fail to do these two things leads to partaking in an "unworthy manner."
        (a) Partaking in an "unworthy manner" leads one to "be guilty of the body and blood of the Lord" (11:27), for he "eats and drinks judgment to himself" (11:29).
    4. The Lord's Supper is a most reverent time of concentration, reflection and devotion.

III. Jesus Instituted the Lord's Supper to Be Observed By the Church _____.
A. Division exists over the frequency of observing the Lord's Supper.
    1. Some groups partake weekly, some monthly, some quarterly, some annually. For some, it is left up to the discretion of the leadership to determine frequency.
    2. It is obvious that God did not give different commands to each of these groups, but that they are making these choices on their own. Do they have the right to do that?

3. Does the Bible give any direction in this matter of frequency? Or does it leave the door wide open? If God is not specific as to frequency, then observing it once during your life would be enough.

B. God did give very clear instructions on the regularity and frequency of partaking.
   1. By reading the books of Acts and First Corinthians, God's authority is understood.
   2. Readers are confronted with apostolic instruction and apostolic example.
   3. What the apostles taught and practiced in one church is what they taught and practiced in every church (1 Cor. 4:17; 7:17; 14:33; 16:1; cf. 2 Thess. 2:15).

C. The New Testament church _____ in the Lord's Supper.
   1. "And they continued steadfastly...in the breaking of bread" (Acts 2:42).
   2. "The breaking of bread" is a reference to the Lord's Supper (when Jesus broke bread).
   3. In the Greek, there is a definite article "the" before "breaking" and before "bread."
      (a) This was a specific breaking (feast) of a specific bread (the Lord's Supper).
   4. "They continued steadfastly" is made up of two separate Greek verbs.
      (a) "They were" is in the Greek imperfect tense, indicating a habitual practice.
      (b) "Continued steadfastly" is in the present tense, indicating continual practice.
   5. There was definitely a regularity and frequency to the Lord's Supper.
      (a) If God did not specify the exact frequency, then it might be left to man to decide.
      (b) However, we must let the Bible speak before we speak.

D. The New Testament church _____ the Lord's Supper (on Sunday).
   1. In Acts 20:7 is an example of the church coming together to eat the Lord's Supper.
      (a) "Now on the first day of the week, when the disciples came together to break bread."
      (b) The day of the week is specified. Why specify the day if it didn't matter?
         (1) Though in a hurry, Paul had waited seven days just for this occasion (20:6).
      (c) "When" ties the day with the gathering as an established and expected practice.
      (d) "Came together" is passive, indicating it was initiated by God and not themselves.
      (e) "To break bread" is an infinitive of purpose, indicating their reason for gathering.
      (f) Acts 20:7 is an approved example for the church today to follow.
         (1) There is apostolic approval (and teaching) for the expectation and practice.
         (2) The Troas church was practicing what every church practiced.
         (3) What was taught to and practiced in one church was universal (see III, B, 3).
      (g) The gathering for worship & the breaking of bread occurred at the same frequency.
         (1) If the frequency of one could be changed, the frequency of the other could be also.
   2. In 1 Corinthians 11:17-34 is direction to the church to come together for the Lord's Supper.
      (a) The context is about when the church would "come together" (11:17, 18, 20, 33, 34).
      (b) In disapproval for their practice and to return them to the proper way, Paul said, "When you come together in one place, it is not to eat the Lord's Supper" (11:20).
         (1) In other words, they were supposed to be gathering to eat the Lord's Supper.
         (2) But, the supper they were gathering to eat was NOT the "Lord's" (v. 20-22).
         (3) They had corrupted the Lord's Supper and, thus, corrupted the worship.
      (c) The early church was supposed to be "coming together" to worship (14:23-25), to edify (14:26) and to eat the Lord's Supper (11:20, 33).
      (d) The gathering for worship & the Lord's Supper was to occur at the same frequency.
         (1) If the frequency of one could be changed, the frequency of the other could be also.
      (e) Thus, it should not be surprising that God urges Christians, "...not forsaking the assembling of ourselves together, as is the manner of some" (Heb. 10:25).

E. The New Testament church came together _____.

1. When God instructed Israel, "Remember the Sabbath day, to keep it holy" (Ex. 20:8), which Sabbath do you suppose they understood God to be identifying?
   (a) The obvious answer is that they understood He meant every Sabbath, every week.
2. In 1 Corinthians 16:1-2 is instruction to gather every first day of the week.
   (a) The orders being given were the same orders to all churches (16:1; cf. 4:17; 7:17).
   (b) The NASB & ESV properly translate verse 2: "On the first day of every week."
      (1) The Greek word *kata* (meaning "every") is in this verse.
      (2) Even if *kata* was not in this verse, which weeks have first days? Every one!
   (c) Churches were given instructions about their weekly gatherings on Sundays.
      (1) This was their common practice, as taught to them by the apostles.
   (d) Question: How often do "churches" today take up a collection?
      (1) Answer: Every Sunday! Why? Because 1 Corinthians 16:1-2 teaches it.
      (2) But, why not partake of the Lord's Supper, which is the purpose of gathering?

F. Put all of the evidence together:
   1. The New Testament church continued steadfastly in the Lord's Supper. (There was a regularity and frequency to its observation.)
   2. The New Testament church came together for the purpose of eating the Lord's Supper. (This was the focus of their assembly.)
   3. The New Testament church came together every first day of the week. (This was "the Lord's Day"—the day they assembled as His body.)
   4. Therefore, the New Testament church continued steadfastly in coming together to eat the Lord's Supper every first day of the week. The sum of God's Word is truth!
   5. How can the church today do any different, any more or any less?

IV. Jesus Instituted the Lord's Supper to Be _____.
A. The Lord makes a definite distinction between the Lord's Supper and a common meal.
   1. In the worship context of Acts 2:42, the definite article "the" specifies the communion.
      (a) Later, in Acts 2:46, the church was "breaking bread" in a common meal.
   2. In Acts 20:7, the breaking of bread was the communion of the whole church.
      (a) Later, in Acts 20:11, Paul (single pronoun "he") ate a common meal.
   3. In 1 Corinthians 11, the church was making the communion a common meal (20-21).
      (a) Verse 33 specifies that they were to come together to eat the Lord's Supper.
      (b) Verse 34 specifies that the common meals could be enjoyed at home.
B. The Lord identifies those for whom the Lord's Supper is intended.
   1. Jesus promised to partake in the Lord's Supper "in the kingdom of God" (Mk. 14:25).
   2. Jesus observes the communion "with" those in His "Father's kingdom" (Matt. 26:29).
   3. Therefore, the Lord's Supper is for citizens in the kingdom of God (John 3:5).
   4. However, Scripture gives no authority for practicing "open" or "closed communion."

V. Conclusion
A. The Lord's Supper was instituted by Jesus to be an integral part of Christian worship.
   1. It is a communion, a memorial, a proclamation, and a time of examination.
B. The Lord's Supper was instituted by Jesus to be observed every first day of the week.
C. The Lord's Supper is "the Lord's," and He alone has authority to regulate it.
D. There is no authority in Scripture to observe the Lord's Supper:
   1. On a different day than the first day of the week.
   2. On a different frequency than every week, on the first day of every week.
   3. On a different occasion than the worship assembly of the church (like a wedding).
E. May we commune with Him every Sunday—remembering Him and examining ourselves.

Lesson 10: Music in the Worship of the Church

I. **All Worship Must Be _____ to Be Acceptable to Him!**
   A. True worshipers worship God "in spirit and in truth" (John 4:24).
   B. To worship in truth is to worship according to His divine standard, His word (John 17:17).
   C. God is the author and object of worship, therefore, He is the only one who has the authority to determine what is acceptable and unacceptable in worship (John 4:23-24).
   D. All that we say and do (including in worship) must be by His authority (Col. 3:17).

II. **All Worship Today Must Be Authorized By the New Testament!**
   A. The church is a New Testament institution of God (Matt. 16:18; Acts 2:47; 20:28).
      1. The church must follow the N.T. as its sole authority (Matt. 17:5; Col. 3:17).
   B. The Old Testament (with its worship) is no longer binding or an authority for man today.
      1. It was abrogated by the death of Christ (Col. 2:14-17) and the giving of the N.T. (Jer. 31:31-34; Heb. 8:8-13; 9:15-17). We are no longer under it (Gal. 3:19-25).
      2. Therefore, we cannot use it to justify or authorize worship practices (Gal. 5:1-4).
   C. See Lesson 2 for more on the Two Covenants and the abrogation of the Old Testament.

III. **God Desires and Has Authorized _____ in Worship!**
   A. The New Testament identifies and authorizes the _____ in worship—singing.
      1. Music in worship in the New Testament was only singing.
      2. Every N.T. verse referencing music in worship is always singing (Mt. 26:30; Mk. 14:26; Acts 16:25; Rom. 15:9; 1 Cor. 14:15; Eph. 5:19; Col. 3:16; Heb. 2:12; 13:15; Jas. 5:13).
   B. The New Testament identifies and authorizes the object of singing in worship—God.
      1. By example, our singing is to be directed "to God" (Acts 16:25).
      2. By instruction, our singing is to be directed "to the Lord" (Eph. 5:19; Col. 3:16).
      3. Jesus Himself sings in the assembly "to You," the Lord (Heb. 2:12).
   C. The New Testament identifies and authorizes the two-fold purpose of singing.
      1. Our singing is to render praise & thanksgiving to God (Rom. 15:9; Heb. 13:15; Jas. 5:13).
      2. Our singing is to speak to, teach and admonish one another (Eph. 5:19; Col. 3:16).
   D. The New Testament identifies and authorizes the manner in which to sing.
      1. We are to sing "with the spirit" (1 Cor. 14:15). Our hearts must be engaged!
         (a) "...making melody in your heart" (Eph. 5:19); "...with grace in your hearts" (Col. 3:16).
      2. We are to sing "with the understanding" (1 Cor. 14:15). Our minds must be engaged!
   E. The New Testament identifies and authorizes _____ to be used in singing.
      1. There is an instrument authorized and demanded by God in N.T. worship.
      2. However, God does not authorize a mechanical instrument in N.T. worship.
      3. God does authorize and demand the instrument of the heart in N.T. worship.
      4. "...singing and making melody in your heart to the Lord" (Eph. 5:19).
   F. God alone can and does authorize acceptable worship, and He authorizes singing.
      1. Notice that God nowhere identifies or authorizes mechanical instruments in worship.
      2. Our worship can fulfill every desire and command of God, and our worship can impart every benefit God had in mind for the worshiper, without a mechanical instrument.

IV. **God Is _____ (Not Generic) About Singing in Worship.**
   A. God authorizes through both generic authority and specific authority.
      1. Virtually every authorized command in the Bible has both generic & specific elements.
         (a) Specific commands set forth the specific manner in which God's ordinances are to be implemented (without addition, subtraction or substitution).
            (1) This means there is uniformity as all obey the same commands.

(2) The specific element of the command rules out all other possible specifics.

(b) Generic commands set forth the general manner in which God's ordinances are to be implemented, leaving the specifics to the judgment of the individual.

(1) The generic element gives liberty, where there may be a diversity of practice.

(2) Of course, no liberty can violate another of God's commands.

B. It is vital to understand the difference between generic authority and specific authority, and to understand how each includes inclusive and exclusive elements.

1. A physician can give a prescription to a pharmacist that is generic or specific.

(a) Generic Prescription: "Give the patient an antibiotic."

(1) Inclusive: ANY antibiotic, any dosage and any frequency would be permitted.

(2) Exclusive: ALL other kinds of drugs (antacids, laxatives, steroids, etc.).

(b) Specific Prescription: "Give the patient 250mg of tetracycline twice a day."

(1) Inclusive: ONLY tetracycline, but any brand would be permitted.

(2) Exclusive: ALL other antibiotics, dosages, frequencies are prohibited.

(3) The very thing included in the Generic Command is excluded in the Specific.

(4) By specifying the type of antibiotic, the physician automatically (without saying another word) excludes every other type of antibiotic. A thing does not have to be specifically forbidden to be unauthorized.

C. God utilized Generic Authority and Specific Authority in the commands of the Bible.

1. God told Noah, "Make yourself an ark of gopherwood..." (Gen. 6:14-16).

(a) Inclusive: ANY tools needed to build (hammer, saw, etc.) would be permitted.

(b) Inclusive: ONLY gopherwood, but any length/width of boards would be permitted.

(c) Exclusive: ALL other kinds of wood are prohibited.

(d) By specifying the type of wood, God automatically (without saying another word) excluded every other type of wood. A thing does not have to be specifically forbidden to be unauthorized.

(e) God's commands were to be obeyed, without addition or subtraction.

2. God commands Christians to partake of the Lord's Supper with unleavened bread and fruit of the vine every Sunday in their "come together" assembly (Matt. 26:26-29; Acts 20:7; 1 Cor. 11:17-26; 16:1-2; Heb. 10:25).

(a) Inclusive: ANY building, tent, home, owned, rented, etc. are permitted.

(b) Inclusive: ONLY unleavened bread and fruit of the vine are permitted.

(c) Exclusive: ALL other kinds of "food" (meat, apples, soda, etc.) are prohibited.

(d) Inclusive: ANY time on Sunday (6:00 a.m., 6:00 p.m., etc.) is permitted.

(e) Inclusive: ONLY the first day of every week (Sunday) is permitted.

(f) Exclusive: ALL other days or frequencies.

(g) By specifying the "food" and the day of the week, God automatically (without saying another word) excluded every other type of "food" and every other day. A thing does not have to be specifically forbidden to be unauthorized.

D. Regarding music in worship, God specified singing: "...singing and making melody in your heart to the Lord" (Eph. 5:19).

1. Inclusive: Words, tunes, pitch, 4-part harmony, 4/4 time, multiple verses, etc.

2. Inclusive: Books, projectors, starting note/pitch, beating time, etc.

3. Inclusive: ONLY singing as a congregation is permitted.

4. Exclusive: ALL other kinds of music are prohibited.

(a) There are two kinds of music: instrumental and vocal.

(b) God could have used Generic Authority and commanded, "Make music."

(1) If He had, then singing, playing or singing-and-playing would be permitted.

(2) And, a diversity of those practices would be authorized and expected.

(c) However, God chose to specify (and command) the type of music in worship.

(d) By specifying the "music" in Christian worship, God automatically (without saying another word) excluded every other type of "music." A thing does not have to be specifically forbidden to be unauthorized.

(e) Just like the examples above (prescriptions, wood for the ark, etc.), when the spoken words specify a particular item/action in a category, all other items/actions in that category are automatically excluded.

E. We readily understand generic/specific and inclusive/exclusive in every part of life. Why do those same basic principles not readily apply singing in worship? They must. They do.

V. God Is _____ in Worship.

A. A favorite argument in favor of instrumental music in worship is, "There isn't a verse in the Bible that says, 'Thou shalt not use instrumental music in worship.'"

1. On the surface, one must admit that this is true. No such verse can be found.

2. This is referred to as "the silence of the Scriptures."

B. So, how is one to properly handle the silence of the Scriptures?

1. If a teaching or practice is not explicitly forbidden, is it permitted or prohibited?

C. This is not a hard issue, for we readily understand "silence" in everyday life.

1. When a parent sends a child to the store for milk and bread, is it permissible to buy M&M's and Coke, since mom didn't say, "You may not buy M&M's and Coke"?

2. When a boy gets in trouble for being in a Ladies' Restroom, is it permissible for him to be in there and stay in there, since the sign didn't say, "No boys or men allowed"?

3. When a music tutor says, "Sing the National Anthem," is it permissible for her student to play it, since the tutor did not say, "Do not play the National Anthem"?

4. When God is "silent" about instrumental music, why don't the same common-sense principles apply? They must. They do.

D. God understands the significance of silence and makes arguments based upon it.

1. The superiority of Jesus over angels is argued from silence (Heb. 1:4-5, 13).

(a) The Bible never said to an angel, "You are My Son...Sit at My right hand..."

(b) God's penman made an argument based on something the Bible did NOT say.

2. The superiority of Jesus as High Priest and the necessity of the change of the law is argued from silence (Heb. 7:11-15).

(a) Jesus could not serve as a priest on earth (Heb. 8:4), because He was of the tribe of Judah and not the priestly tribe of Levi, as specified of God (Heb. 7:14).

(b) Jesus "arose from Judah, of which tribe Moses spoke nothing concerning priesthood."

(1) When God specified Levi, He was silent regarding the other tribes.

(2) His silence was not permissible, to allow any other tribe to be the priests.

(3) His silence was prohibitive. Even Jesus could not be a priest from Judah.

(c) The only way for Jesus to be High Priest was to change the law.

(1) The only way to make God's silence permissible today is to change His law.

E. God's "silence" regarding instrumental music in worship is _____!

1. Scripture is also "silent" about infant baptism, worshiping saints, praying to Mary, counting beads, burning incense, animal sacrifices, lighting candles for the dead, etc.

(a) "Where is the verse that says not to do these things? God doesn't say 'not to.'"

(b) Is the church permitted to add anything it likes to a perceived "silence" of God?

2. Christians must "do all in the name of the Lord Jesus" (Col. 3:17).

(a) The music that God authorizes in N.T. worship involves "speaking," "singing," "making melody in the heart," "giving thanks," "teaching," "admonishing," "praise," "declare/tell/proclaim," etc. (Eph. 5:19-20; Col. 3:16; Heb. 2:12; 13:15).

    (1) All of these are uniquely accomplished in singing.

    (2) None of these can be fulfilled with instruments of music.

(b) We have no right to go beyond what is written (1 Cor. 4:6; 2 John 9)!

(c) We have no right to add to the word of God (Rev. 22:18; Deut. 4:2; 12:32).

F. Severe consequences await those who do not respect the silence of the Scriptures.
1. Nadab and Abihu offered "unauthorized fire before the Lord" (Lev. 10:1-2).
2. God specified that fire was to be obtained "from off the altar" (Lev. 16:12; Num. 16:46).
3. Nadab and Abihu took fire from a source, "which He had not commanded them" (v.1).
4. God was silent regarding that other fire, but His silence was prohibitive.
5. Because they did not respect the silence of God, but treated it as permissible rather than prohibitive, "fire went out from the Lord and devoured them" (10:2).

G. Conclusion: To act in a realm where the Lord is silent is prohibitive and sinful!
1. Where's the verse that says not to play an instrument? It's the one that says to sing!

VI. Answering Some Common Arguments Made to Support Instrumental Music in Worship.

A. Some argue that instruments are permissible because God accepted them in the O.T.
1. We are no longer under the O.T. (Gal. 3:19-25), for it was nailed to the cross (Col. 2:14).
2. To bring one part of O.T. into N.T. worship demands bringing it all (Gal. 5:3), including animal sacrifices, burning incense, three annual trips to Jerusalem, etc. (See II.)

B. Some argue that instruments are permissible because they are found in heaven.
1. First of all, remember that Revelation is written in signs/figurative language (Rev. 1:1).
2. The same verse mentions "golden bowls full of incense" (5:8). Are those permitted?
3. There is also a "white horse" in heaven (Rev. 19:11). Are those permitted in worship?
4. Something figurative in heaven is not authorization from God for His church on earth!

C. Some argue that instruments are just an aid, like a tuning fork or pitch pipe.
1. When we use a tuning fork, song book or projector, we've done nothing but sing.
2. When an instrument is used, now there has been singing + playing (two kinds of music).
3. This is an unauthorized addition, because it is another kind of music (Rev. 22:18-19).

D. Some argue that the Greek word *psallo* means "to play."
1. *Psallo* varied in meaning over time (like "gay," "bad," "sick" and "cell" today).
2. At times, it did mean "to pluck," like a harp string, a carpenter's string or bowstring.
3. However, in N.T. times, lexical scholars and translators affirm that it meant "to sing."
4. Even if it did mean "to pluck," God specifies the instrument – the heart!
5. If it means "to play," then it is a command, and it is not optional & everyone must play.

E. Some argue that they have a "God-given talent" for playing, so it must be acceptable.
1. Will all talents be permitted, like dancing, juggling, yodeling, chugging, cooking, etc.?
2. Is worship intended as a talent show for God? If so, why did He give parameters for it?
3. God is the object of worship, not us! God is the director of worship, not us!

VII. Conclusion

A. In the New Testament, God specifies, authorizes and commands singing in worship.
B. The New Testament does not authorize the use of mechanical instruments in worship.
1. To use mechanical instruments in worship is to add to God's Word (Rev. 22:18).
2. Therefore, the use of mechanical instruments in worship is unauthorized and sinful.
C. God alone has the right to authorize, and man must submit humbly to His revealed will.
D. Worship is TO God as authorized BY God! May we obey His will, in order to please Him!

Lesson 11: The Role of Women in the Church

I. **The Role of Women in the Church Is an Important, But Sensitive Subject.**

    A. Some individuals may not even know why this subject needs to be studied and taught.

    B. Some individuals may be offended that this subject is being studied and taught.

    C. The reality is that "the role of women in the church" is a Bible subject, therefore, it must be studied and taught. But, we must limit ourselves to what the Bible says about it.

    D. Some churches of Christ are struggling with this subject.

        1. "Can women serve in the same leadership roles in the worship service as the men?"

        2. "Can women serve in the same leadership roles within the church as the men?"

        3. "Why should women be considered in a different light than the men?"

    E. These are questions that some churches are trying to answer.

        1. The key to all of this is, "What does God's Word say?" That's all that matters.

        2. The church belongs to Him. The Bible is His "manual" for the church.

        3. Rather than look to tradition or culture or current trends, we must look to His Word!

II. **God Has Designed Both _____ in Men and Women.**

    A. God made men and women to be _____.

        1. The source for each was different—"dust" (Gen. 2:7) and a "rib" (Gen. 2:21-22).

        2. The sexuality for each was different—a "man" (Gen. 2:8) and a "woman" (Gen. 2:22).

        3. The scope of each was different—"tend" (Gen. 2:15) and "helper" (Gen. 2:18).

        4. These differences in NO WAY imply a difference in worth, value or ability.

        5. It should not surprise us, then, if God gave different roles to each in the church.

    B. God made men and women to be _____.

        1. This may seem like a contradiction with the first point, but it is not.

        2. Men and women are equal in regard to God's love (1 John 4:7-19).

        3. Men and women are equal in regard to God's salvation (Gal. 3:28; Acts 5:14; 8:12).

            (a) Everyone who is "in Christ" has the same status before God. They are all equally "children" and equally "in Christ" (Gal. 3:26-28).

            (b) Everyone who is "in Christ" has the same privileges from God. They are all equally saved, all have access to Him through prayer, all are one (Eph. 2:1-22).

            (c) But, the same status and the same privileges do not imply the same function.

        4. Men and women are equal in regard to God's promise of heaven (1 Pet. 3:7).

            (a) They are "heirs together of the grace of life."

            (b) No man or woman has more right to eternal life based upon their gender.

            (c) But, this does not imply that they are to have equal roles in the church.

    C. God gave men and women _____ in the church.

        1. Before we examine those roles, we need to understand the nature of different roles.

        2. Having different roles does NOT suggest that one is superior and one is inferior.

            (a) God has always held women in high regard, never seeing an inferior (see Prov. 31).

            (b) Women were an integral part of His scheme of redemption (Gal. 4:4; Gen. 3:15).

            (c) Some of the greatest people in Bible history were women: Sarah, Rachel, Deborah, Hannah, Ruth, Esther, Mary, Elizabeth, Mary-and-Martha, Lois, Eunice, Priscilla, etc.

            (d) Jesus gave great attention, favor and commendation to women: the Samaritan woman, Mary-and-Martha, Mary Magdalene, widow of Nain, His own mother, etc.

            (e) In a school, the teacher is not inferior to the principal or the school board. They all have different roles, but it is not a superior-inferior relationship.

            (f) The same is true in the organization of the church.

3. Having different roles does NOT mean any preferential treatment is being shown.
   (a) God makes a distinction between elders and deacons (1 Tim. 3:1-13).
   (b) God makes a distinction between elders and members (1 Pet. 5:1-3; Heb. 13:17).
   (c) God makes a distinction between elders and single men (1 Tim. 3:2; Tit. 1:6).
   (d) God makes a distinction between widows to support and not support (1 Ti. 5:3-16).
   (e) God is not unjustly discriminating in any of these examples, nor is He unjustly discriminating by giving men and women different roles in the church.
4. For a man to teach what the Bible says about different roles is not discrimination, as long as he is faithfully teaching God's truth (and doing so with a Christ-like attitude).

III. **God Has _____ in the Church for Men and Women.**
   A. The book of First Timothy was written to give instructions on proper "conduct" in the "house of God, which is the church of the living God" (1 Tim. 3:15).
   B. God specified the roles of _____ for the men in the church.
      1. God specified men to be leaders in the church as elders (1 Tim. 3:2).
      2. God specified men to be leaders in the church as deacons (1 Tim. 3:11-12).
      3. God specified men to be leaders in the worship of the church (1 Tim. 2:8).
         (a) The Greek word for "men" in 1 Timothy 2:8 *(aner)* is exclusively male.
         (b) The men are to lead in the acts of worship, including praying (see verses 1-7).
         (c) The men are to lead "in every place" the church assembles to worship (cf. 1 Co. 1:2).
      4. When God specifies, we must pay attention and follow His instructions.
   C. God specified the role of _____ for the women in the church.
      1. The Greek word for "women" used in 1 Timothy 2 *(gune)* is exclusively female.
      2. Women are called to "learn in silence with all submission" (1 Tim. 2:11).
         (a) In the context of worship in 1 Corinthians 14, women are to "be submissive" (14:34).
      3. The "silence/quietness" in 1 Timothy 2:11 is not total silence (cf. Acts 21:40-22:2).
         (a) The "silence" is a quiet spirit, an attitude of attentiveness and receptiveness.
         (b) It would be difficult for them to participate in worship if they could not speak at all.
      4. The "submission" is a subjecting or subordinating of herself, recognizing her role.
         (a) The word denotes a voluntary choice to place oneself under the authority of another.
         (b) This has nothing to do with one's value or worth, or of being controlled by another.
         (c) Compare this again to the submission of a teacher to a principal. The emphasis is on roles and responsibilities, not on value, superiority or discrimination.
         (d) The context (1 Tim. 2; 1 Cor. 14) is within the church and in its assemblies.
      5. Women are not permitted "to teach or to exercise authority over a man" (1 Tim. 2:12).
         (a) Note first what this does not mean:
            (1) This does not prohibit women from all teaching (see Titus 2:3-5).
            (2) This does not prohibit women from ever teaching a man (see Acts 18:26).
            (3) This does not prohibit women from all teaching in the assembly (see Col. 3:16).
         (b) This is addressing the position of authority inherent in teaching and leading.
            (1) Public leading and teaching subordinates hearers to the speaker.
            (2) The position of the teacher or preacher is a position of authority over hearers.
            (3) For a woman to teach over a man in the church is to violate this passage.
            (4) For a woman to exercise authority over a man in the church (by speaking, praying, standing before the church, serving as an elder, etc.) violates this passage.
         (c) In 1 Corinthians 14:34-35, Paul affirms that:
            (1) Women "are not permitted to speak" in the assembly of the churches.
            (2) "It is shameful for women to speak" in the assembly of the churches.

D. God did not authorize women to serve as _____.
   1. God plainly disclosed His qualifications for one to be appointed as an elder or deacon.
      (a) He must be "married" (1 Tim. 3:2, 12), therefore, a bachelor cannot serve.
      (b) He must have "children" (1 Tim. 3:4, 12), therefore, a childless man cannot serve.
      (c) He must be "the husband of one wife" (1 Tim. 3:2, 12; Tit. 1:6), therefore, a woman cannot serve as an elder or deacon.
   2. God used the exclusive terms again in these passages.
      (a) The elder is to be an *aner* – the Greek word exclusively for male, in contrast to female (1 Tim. 3:2; Tit. 1:6).
      (b) The deacon is to be an *aner* (1 Tim. 3:12).
      (c) The spouses of these men are to be *gune* – the Greek word exclusively for female, in contrast to male (1 Tim. 3:2, 11, 12; Tit. 1:6).
   3. God has a Divine order, which man (or woman) has no right to change.

IV. God Has Provided _____ for the Different Roles of Men and Women.
   A. First of all, we must recognize that God does not have to provide man with an explanation.
      1. When God gives instructions, man just needs to obey them.
      2. When God gives specifications, man just needs to accept them.
      3. Man's acceptance and obedience are not contingent on an explanation from God.
      4. He is the Father. We are the children. He is not obligated to give us a reason.
   B. However, in the matter of the role of women in the church, He gives clear reasoning.
      1. What we will see is that God's rationale has nothing to do with any given culture.
      2. What we will see is that God's rationale has nothing to do with male chauvinism.
      3. God's rationale transcends all culture, all civilizations and all locales for all time.
   C. God provides at least four reasons for His specified role for women in the church.
   D. Reason #1: The _____ of headship/authority (1 Cor. 11:3).
      1. God has an order of authority.
      2. The word "head" (1 Cor. 11:3) is not about source but authority (the Divine order).
      3. A woman is "under the authority" of men. That is God's order of authority.
      4. Women are not inferior to men any more than Christ is inferior to God.
      5. This Divine order was to find universal practice for all time.
         (a) "As <u>in all the churches</u> of the saints, the women should keep silent" (1 Co. 14:33-34).
         (b) "I desire therefore that the men pray <u>everywhere</u>" (1 Tim. 2:8).
   E. Reason #2: The _____ derived from _____ (1 Tim. 2:13; 1 Cor. 11:3, 7-12).
      1. The Divine order of headship is tied to the order of creation, which is not cultural.
         (a) The first word in 1 Timothy 2:13 ("For") will show the Divine reason for verses 8-12.
         (b) Many argue today against the Bible's "restrictions" on women, stating that Paul was just dealing with the culture of the day and that our culture is different today.
         (c) Perhaps (but not successfully) such an argument could be made if verses 13-14 were not in First Timothy. But, those verses forever eliminate the cultural argument.
         (d) Paul ties the role of women in his day (and every day) all the way back to creation.
         (e) God's Divine order goes back to "the beginning of the creation" (Mark 10:6).
      2. God created the male first (giving him chronological priority in the creation) (1 Ti. 2:13).
         (a) God did this to emphasize man's functional purpose and responsibility as head/leader in the home and church. (Priority does not mean superiority.)
      3. God created the woman second (1 Tim. 2:13).
         (a) Woman was specifically designed and created (from the beginning) for the purpose of being a subordinate, companion-helper, suited for man (not inferior).

4. God's creation order has intentional purpose (1 Cor. 11:8-9).
   (a) God could have created the woman first or both simultaneously, but He did not.
   (b) God's order was intended to convey His will regarding gender roles.
   (c) God gave spiritual teaching to Adam before Eve was created (Gen. 2:15-17).
   (d) God created the female as "an help meet for him" (Gen. 2:18, 20).
   (e) Man was not "created for the woman, but woman for the man" (1 Cor. 11:9).
F. Reason #3: The _____ into the world (1 Tim. 2:14).
   1. Eve led humanity into sin (when she took the spiritual initiative over the man).
      (a) The nature of Eve's sin is that she was "deceived," but Adam "was not deceived."
      (b) Eve believed Satan's lie that she might become as God—she was "beguiled."
   2. In the punishment for her sin, God reaffirmed to the woman her role of submission to her husband (Gen. 3:16). Her subjection was increased because of her sin.
G. Reason #4: The relation of _____ (Eph. 5:23-33).
   1. God likens the husband-wife relationship to the Christ-church relationship.
   2. The husband is the "head" of the wife, as Christ is the "head" of the church (5:23).
   3. The wife is to "submit" to her husband as "the church submits to Christ" (5:22, 24).
   4. No more should a wife think of exercising authority over her husband than the church should think of exercising authority over Christ. The parallel is key to this passage.

V. God Has Given Wonderful Roles for Women to Fulfill in the Home and in the Church.
A. Christian women are wonderfully talented servants in the church with enormous capabilities.
B. There are many meaningful roles that godly women can and do fulfill in service to Christ.
   1. In the home (this is not an exhaustive list by any means):
      (a) "...bear children, manage the house, give no opportunity to the adversary" (1 Ti. 5:14).
      (b) "...love their husbands [and] children...be sensible, pure, workers at home" (Tit. 2:4-5).
   2. In the church (this is not an exhaustive list by any means):
      (a) "be...teachers of good things" (Tit. 2:3).
      (b) Teach other women (Tit. 2:3-5) and teach children (2 Tim. 3:14-15).
      (c) Teach alongside men (Acts 18:26; Phil. 4:3).
      (d) Help to administer church programs (Rom. 16:1-2).
      (e) Do good works for others (Acts 9:36).
      (f) Show hospitality (Acts 12:12; 16:14; 1 Tim. 5:10).
      (g) Continue in prayer for the church and all its members (Acts 1:14).

VI. Conclusion
A. There are God-given differences between males and females.
B. God has designed specific roles for each one to have in His order, and each one is pleasing to God when he/she fulfills his/her God-given roles.
C. A Christian (man or woman) should not insist upon exercising his/her "rights."
D. The only "rights" a Christian has are the ones given by God.
E. God has commanded all Christians to be in subjection to Him.
F. A woman must obey all the commands of God, as surely as any man must.
G. Submission has nothing to do with quality or worth, but it is based upon God's order.
H. The role of women in the church is not cultural, but it is universal, being tied to creation.
I. For a woman to exercise authority over men in the church violates the principle of subjection.
J. The role of women in the church is not a matter of control, power or oppression.
   1. It is a matter of submission on the part of ALL to the will of God (Eph. 5:21; Jas. 4:7).
   2. It is a matter of willingness on the part of ALL to subordinate themselves to the Divine arrangement regarding sexes and roles.

Lesson 12: The Person, Process & Purpose of Baptism

Fundamentals
of the Faith

I. The Subject of Baptism Is Vitally Important and Yet Highly Controversial.
   A. The subject of baptism is mentioned more than 100 times in the New Testament.
   B. If it were not for the New Testament, man would know nothing of the topic or practice.
   C. Man finds all that he can and needs to know about this subject within his New Testament.
   D. The subject is vitally important for us, for it comes to us from God Himself.
   E. Yet, baptism is one of the most controversial topics, as people have different ideas about "who" should be baptized, "what" baptism is and "why" a person is to be baptized.
   F. Seeing that the idea of baptism comes from heaven (Matt. 21:25), and seeing that the authority of Christ commanded baptism (Matt. 28:18-20), and seeing that the Word of Christ will judge us in the end (John 12:48), let's simply examine what the Bible says.

II. The Bible Specifies That There Is _____.
   A. The New Testament mentions several baptisms in the gospel accounts and the book of Acts.
   B. But, when the book of Ephesians was written, there was then only "one baptism" (4:5).
   C. Which baptism, mentioned in the New Testament, is the "one baptism"?
      1. It is not "the baptism of John," for that baptism was to prepare for the coming of Christ (John 3:26-30) and was not "in the name of the Lord Jesus" (Acts 19:3-5).
      2. It is not "the baptism of the Holy Spirit," for that was a baptism administered only by the Lord Himself, not man (Matt. 3:11; John 1:33); it involved receiving a promise rather than obeying a command (Luke 24:49; Acts 1:4-8; 2:1-4); and, there are only two instances of this baptism recorded in Scripture (Acts 2 and Acts 10).
      3. It is not "the baptism of sufferings," for that was fulfilled in Christ's death and the persecution of the saints that followed (Matt. 22:22-23; Mark 10:38-39; Luke 12:50).
      4. It is not "the baptism of fire," for that is the eternal fires of hell yet to come (Matt. 3:11; Luke 3:16).
      5. The "ONE baptism" is water baptism of Christ's Great Commission.
         (a) It is the universal baptism for all mankind (Matt. 28:19; Mark 16:15).
         (b) It is the baptism that is commanded to be obeyed (Matt. 28:19; Acts 10:48).
         (c) It is the baptism administered by man (Matt. 28:19; Acts 8:38).
         (d) It is the baptism administered in water (Acts 8:36-39; 10:47; 1 Pet. 3:20-31).
         (e) It is the baptism done "in the name of the Lord Jesus" (Acts 2:38; 10:48; 19:5).
   D. This one baptism of Christ must be studied, understood and obeyed.

III. The Bible Specifies the _____ Who Is the Biblical _____ for Baptism.
   A. The person who is baptized must meet certain Biblical conditions before baptism:
      1. One must be taught the gospel (Matt. 28:19-20; Mark 16:15-16).
      2. One must gladly receive the gospel (Acts 2:41).
      3. One must believe the gospel (Mark 16:16; Acts 8:12-13, 36-37; 16:31-33).
      4. One must be convicted of sins (Acts 2:37).
      5. One must repent of sins (Acts 2:38).
      6. One must knowingly acknowledge (confess) his faith (Acts 8:36-38).
      7. One must desire (and need) to fulfill the purpose of baptism in his/her own life (see Roman numeral V below).
      8. One must be prepared for the commitment that baptism requires (Rom. 6:4; Gal. 3:27; 2 Cor. 5:17; 1 Cor. 15:58).
   B. Only those who meet these conditions can be Scripturally (and properly) baptized.
   C. If a person does not (or cannot) meet all of these conditions, he/she is not a candidate.

D. Therefore, it is readily apparent that infants are not Scriptural candidates for baptism.
   1. Infants do not and cannot meet the conditions for baptism listed above.
   2. The fact is that infants have no need to be baptized, for they are sinless, pure, holy and safe in the eyes of God (Matt. 18:3; 19:14; Luke 18:16-17), and are not born with any inherited sins from their parents or previous generations (Ezek. 18:20).

IV. **The Bible Specifies the _____ That Is the Biblical _____ for Baptism.**
   A. What is the proper mode of baptism? How is baptism to be administered?
      1. Can one be "baptized" only by immersion into water?
      2. Can one be "baptized" only by sprinkling or pouring water?
      3. Or, can one be "baptized" in any of these ways, as long as he is "baptized"?
   B. The Bible very plainly describes what is involved in Bible baptism:
      1. "Much water" is required to be baptized with Bible baptism (John 3:23).
      2. The person being baptized must come "to" the water (Matt. 3:11; Acts 8:36).
      3. The person being baptized and the baptizer must go "down into the water" (Ac. 8:36).
      4. The person being baptized must be "buried...in baptism" (Col. 2:12; Rom. 6:4).
      5. The person being baptized must be "raised" from the water (Rom. 6:4; Col. 2:12).
      6. The person being baptized and the baptizer must come "up out of the water" (Ac. 8:39).
      7. The Bible makes it very clear that baptism is immersion of the body into water.
   C. By simply substituting the words "sprinkling, pouring, immersing" for the word "baptism" or "baptize," the Bible reader can easily understand what baptism is.
      1. All the people "were sprinkled/poured/immersed by [John] in the Jordan" (Mt. 3:6).
      2. "After being sprinkled/poured/immersed, Jesus came up from the water" (Mt. 3:16).
      3. "John also was sprinkling/pouring/immersing in Aenon near Salim, because there was much water there" (John 3:23).
      4. "They went down into the water, and he sprinkled/poured/immersed him" (Acts 8:38).
      5. "We were buried with Him through sprinkling/pouring/immersing into death" (Ro. 6:4).
      6. When substituted for "baptism," immersion makes perfect sense. The others do not.
   D. The Greek verb for "baptize" *(baptizo)* means "to dip, immerse, submerge, overwhelm."
      1. The original word itself specifically means "to immerse."
      2. The original word itself will not allow for "sprinkling" or "pouring" as an option.
   E. When one is baptized, he obeys the "form of doctrine" laid out by Jesus (Rom. 6:17).
      1. The "form" that Jesus left to be followed was a death, burial and resurrection (6:3-4).
      2. In baptism, one "dies to sin" (6:3, 11), is "buried" and is "raised" to a new life (6:4).
   F. Bible baptism is clearly an immersion into water, which all Biblical evidence demands.

V. **The Bible Specifies the _____ That God Assigns to Baptism.**
   A. Suppose that you wrote on a piece of paper, "What is the purpose of baptism?"
      1. Then, suppose you mailed that question to ten different "churches" around town.
      2. Do you suppose that you'd receive the exact same answer from all ten "churches"?
      3. Or, do you suppose that you would receive different and even conflicting answers?
      4. This is a controversial issue because people have differing ideas about baptism's purpose.
      5. Let us put aside our own opinions for a moment, and let us take that same question to the Bible and let the Bible answer—"What is the purpose of baptism?"
   B. According to the Bible, the purpose of baptism is _____.
      1. Jesus commanded His disciples to go and "make disciples" by "baptizing" (Mt. 28:19).
      2. Peter "commanded them to be baptized in the name of the Lord" (Acts 10:47-48).
      3. Baptism is a "must" (Acts 9:6+22:16), in order to obey "the will of God" (Lk. 7:29-30).
      4. Being baptized to obey the command, but not for the right reason, is not Bible baptism.

C. According to the Bible, the purpose of baptism is _____.
   1. Jesus taught, "He who believes and is baptized will be saved" (Mark 16:16).
     (a) The word "and" joins two items of equal grammatical importance.
       (1) "And" means that "believing" is equally as important as being "baptized."
       (2) The end result is not possible without both elements being present.
     (b) Jesus places being "saved" AFTER being "baptized." That is Jesus' order.
       (1) One cannot be saved and then be baptized. That is not Jesus' order.
       (2) One cannot be baptized and then believe. That is not Jesus' order.
   2. Peter emphatically stated, "Baptism does now save us" (1 Pet. 3:21).
D. According to the Bible, the purpose of baptism is _____.
   1. Peter commanded, "Repent, and...be baptized...for the remission of sins..." (Ac. 2:38).
     (a) The Greek word for "for" means "to obtain, in order to" and "denotes purpose."
     (b) "For" means the same thing for "repent" as it does for "be baptized."
   2. This is not man's idea. It is done by the authority of ("in the name of") Jesus Christ.
E. According to the Bible, the purpose of baptism is _____.
   1. Ananias urged Saul, "Arise and be baptized, and wash away your sins" (Acts 22:16).
   2. The washing away of sins is inseparably tied ("and") to baptism.
   3. Even after believing and praying, Saul still had his sins and needed to be baptized.
F. According to the Bible, the purpose of baptism is _____.
   1. In baptism, "sin [is] done away with" and one is "freed from sin" (Rom. 6:3-7, 17-18).
   2. In baptism, one puts "off the body of the sins of the flesh" (Col. 2:11-13).
G. According to the Bible, the purpose of baptism is _____.
   1. Jesus shed His saving blood in His death (John 19:34; Heb. 9:12; 13:12; cf. Rev. 1:5).
   2. In baptism, one is "baptized into His death" (Rom. 6:3), wherein Jesus' blood saves.
H. According to the Bible, the purpose of baptism is _____.
   1. One is baptized "into the name of the Father...Son and...Holy Spirit" (Mt. 28:19, ASV).
   2. The word "into" emphasizes a change of relationship from "outside" a relationship
     with the Godhead to "inside" a relationship with the Godhead. Only in baptism.
I. According to the Bible, the purpose of baptism is _____.
   1. Jesus taught that one "must" be "born of water and the Spirit" (John 3:5, 7).
   2. By (1) "the Spirit" and (2) "water," one can (3) "enter the kingdom of God."
   3. By (1) "the Word" and (2) "washing of water," one is (3) "cleansed" (Eph. 5:26).
   4. By (1) "the Holy Spirit" and (2) "the washing of regeneration," one is (3) "saved" (Tit. 3:5).
   5. Note the parallel in each of these passages, emphasizing the essentiality of baptism.
   6. One is not born again until he follows "the Word" and is baptized in "water."
J. According to the Bible, the purpose of baptism is _____.
   1. Jesus taught, "Unless one is born again, he cannot see the kingdom of God" (Jn. 3:3).
   2. "Unless one is born of water and the Spirit, he cannot enter the kingdom of God" (3:5).
K. According to the Bible, the purpose of baptism is _____.
   1. On Pentecost, about 3,000 were baptized and "added to the church" (Acts 2:41, 47).
   2. In baptism, "we were all baptized into one body" (i.e., the church) (1 Cor. 12:13).
L. According to the Bible, the purpose of baptism is _____.
   1. "Sons of God" are those who "through faith" have been "baptized" (Gal. 3:26-27).
   2. That is the new relationship (cf. Mt. 28:19) obtained when "born again" (John 3:3-7).
M. According to the Bible, the purpose of baptism is _____.
   1. In baptism, one is able to then "put on Christ" (Gal. 3:27).
   2. Before baptism, one does not have Christ!

N. According to the Bible, the purpose of baptism is _____.
    1. The Bible emphatically teaches that "all spiritual blessings are IN CHRIST" (Eph. 1:3).
       (a) IN CHRIST is "the forgiveness of sins" (Eph. 1:7), "an inheritance" (Eph. 1:11), "no condemnation" (Rom. 8:1), "all the promises of God" (2 Cor. 1:20), "a new creation" (2 Cor. 5:17), "salvation" (2 Tim. 2:10), "eternal life" (1 John 5:11), etc.
    2. Only two verses teach how one can get "into Christ" (Rom. 6:3; Gal. 3:27).
    3. Those two verses emphatically teach that baptism is the only one way INTO CHRIST.
    4. Before baptism, one is outside of Christ and deficient of EVERY spiritual blessing.

O. According to the Bible, the purpose of baptism is _____.
    1. "Disciples" are made by being "baptized" (Matt. 28:19), and "disciples" are "called Christians" (Acts 11:26). Therefore, one becomes a Christian by being baptized.
    2. If wearing the name of Paul required being "baptized in the name of Paul," then to wear the name of Christ requires being "baptized in the name of Christ" (1 Cor. 1:12-13).

P. According to the Bible, the purpose of baptism is _____.
    1. In the process of being baptized, one is "calling on the name of the Lord" (Acts 22:16).
    2. The "calls→be saved" in Acts 2:21 is parallel with the "baptized→remission" in 2:38.

Q. According to the Bible, the purpose of baptism is _____.
    1. "Baptism now saves you," for it is "an appeal to God for a good conscience" (1 Pet. 3:21).
    2. Perhaps this is the "calling on the name of the Lord" that is done in baptism.
    3. In baptism, one calls upon God to do "the working" that He promised to do (Col. 2:12).

R. According to the Bible, the purpose of baptism is _____.
    1. Upon baptism, one is "raised" to "walk in newness of life" (Rom. 6:3-4).
    2. When baptized "into Christ," one is "a new creation" with an all-new life (2 Cor. 5:17).

S. According to the Bible, the purpose of baptism is _____.
    1. After two conversions in Acts, it is recorded that both men "rejoiced" (8:39; 16:34).
    2. It is significant that they did not rejoice until AFTER they were baptized.

T. The book of Acts has sometimes been called "The Book of Conversions."
    1. In the Great Commission, Jesus instructed how one can be saved (Matt. 28; Mark 16).
    2. In the Book of Acts, Jesus shows us example after example of people being saved.
    3. In the ten accounts of conversion in Acts, something of great significance is observed.
       (a) The record does not specifically mention that each convert had believed, although we are confident that each one must have believed to be converted.
       (b) But, each one of the accounts specifically records that each person was baptized (2:38, 41; 8:12, 13, 36-38; 9:18; 10:47-48; 16:15, 33; 18:8; 19:5; 22:16).
       (c) If baptism is not essential to salvation, why did God include it in every account?

U. While the Bible is very plain and offers abundant teaching, some still offer objections.
    1. Some appeal to the thief on the cross. But, they should obey the Savior on the cross.
    2. Some point to verses about "believing." But, no verse teaches to "believe only."
    3. Some find verses that don't mention baptism. But, those do not negate ones that do.
    4. Some suggest that salvation is not of works. But, believing is a work (John 6:28-29).
    5. After hearing all the objections, the Bible still teaches that baptism saves from sin.
    6. We cannot pick and choose verses we like. "The sum of Your word is truth" (Ps. 119:160).

VI. Conclusion
A. Baptism is such a wonderful and exciting topic to study!
B. Without the Word of God, we would know nothing about its meaning or its necessity!
C. It is not up to man to decide the place of baptism in God's plan—that's up to God!
D. It is up to man to study, accept and teach the person, process and purpose of Bible baptism!

Lesson 13: The Danger and Reality of Apostasy

I. **A Person Is Saved Only By the Grace of God, But It Is _____.**

    A. The Bible clearly teaches that man is saved from his sins by the grace of God (Eph. 2:1-9; Rom. 3:23-24; 5:15; Tit. 2:11; 3:4-5).

        1. While it is God's grace that saves man, the Bible clearly teaches there are conditions that man must meet in order to be saved (Mark 16:16; Acts 2:38; Eph. 2:8).

    B. The Bible clearly teaches that man, once saved, continues to be saved by the grace of God (1 John 1:6-10; 2:1-2; Eph. 1:7; Rom. 8:34; Heb. 7:25).

        1. While God's grace continues to save, the Bible clearly teaches there are conditions that man must meet to continue to be saved (John 8:31-32; 1 John 1:7-9; Rev. 2:10).

    C. If a lost person fails to meet God's conditions for salvation, he cannot be saved from his sins (John 8:24; Luke 13:3; Matt. 10:33; John 3:3-5).

    D. If a Christian, once saved, fails to continue to meet God's conditions for continued salvation, he cannot continue to be saved from his sins (note "if" in 2 Peter 1:8-10).

        1. This is apostasy—i.e., falling away, turning away from or abandoning faith.

        2. The Scripture teaches that such is possible. A Christian can so sin that he can fall away from God, be separated from God and be lost in sin (again).

    E. The Bible does not teach the man-made doctrine of "once saved, always saved."

    F. In fact, even stronger, the Bible contradicts and crushes the false doctrine again and again.

II. **The Bible Emphatically _____ That One Can Fall Away from God and Lose His Salvation!**

    A. Perhaps the most vivid passage on falling away is in 2 Peter 2:19-22.

        1. Verse 19 teaches, "by what a man is overcome, by this he is enslaved" (NASB).

            (a) Any man can be overcome by something (including sin) and become enslaved.

        2. Verse 20 clearly identifies one who has "escaped the pollutions of the world."

            (a) One who has "escaped the corruption" of the world (cf. 1:4) has been saved.

            (b) They "escaped" the world through the knowledge of Christ as Lord and Savior.

            (c) Note these two words in verse 20: "after" and "again."

                (1) "After they have escaped" – something happens after they are saved.

                (2) "They are again entangled" in the world – like they were before being saved.

                (3) This obviously points to a Christian falling back into sin and separated from God.

        3. "The latter end is worse," for they turned from the truth after obeying it (2:20-22).

        4. Christians can become entangled in the world again and fall away! A vivid truth!

    B. The book of Hebrews, as a whole, teaches that one can fall away, especially 6:4-6.

        1. The writer describes, in vivid terms, individuals who have become Christians: they have "been enlightened...tasted of the heavenly gift...been made partakers of the Holy Spirit...tasted the good word of God and the powers of the age to come" (6:4-5).

            (a) No more beautiful depiction of salvation could be penned.

        2. Then, in the next verse, he continues, "...and then have fallen away" (6:6). Such persons "crucify again for themselves the Son of God, and put Him to an open shame."

        3. Christians can fall away! If they cannot, then this passage is pointless!

    C. The book of Galatians, as a whole, teaches that one can fall away, especially 5:1-4.

        1. Paul is writing to Christians, who have "liberty by which Christ has made us free."

        2. Paul urges these freed Christians not to be "entangled again with a yoke of bondage."

        3. He emphatically affirms that, by "seeking to be justified by law," they had "been severed from Christ" and had "fallen from grace" (5:4).

        4. Christians, once saved, can be lost and severed from Christ! A very clear passage!

D. Jesus' Parable of the Soils teaches that those who are saved can be lost (Luke 8:4-15).
  1. The stony ground folks "hear, receive the word with joy...believe [endure, Matt. 13:21] for a while and in time of temptation fall away" (Luke 8:13).
  2. The thorny ground folks "heard" and became Christians (for they "sprang up" when the seed was planted, 8:6), but their faith is "choked" out and "becomes unfruitful."
  3. Both of these soils (representing people) accepted the word and became Christians, but both of these kinds of people fell away later. It is possible to fall away!
E. Jesus' teaching about the vine and the branches shows the saved can be lost (Jn. 15:1-8).
  1. Jesus taught that each individual follower ("branch") is "in Me" ("in Me" = 6 times).
  2. But, Jesus taught that one "in Me" can so live that God "takes away" that person, and "he is cast out," thrown "into the fire" and "burned" (15:2, 6).
  3. It is possible for one who is saved "in Christ" to fall away and be lost eternally!
F. If a Christian cannot fall away and lose his salvation, then these passages have no meaning.

III. **The Bible Repeatedly _____ That One Can Fall Away from God and Lose His Salvation!**
  A. Paul warns, "Therefore let him who thinks he stands take heed lest he fall" (1 Cor. 10:12).
    1. If a Christian cannot fall away, why was this warning given to Christians?
  B. Hebrews warns, "Beware, brethren, lest there be in any of you an evil heart of unbelief in departing from the living God" (Heb. 3:12).
    1. If a Christian cannot quit believing and depart from God, why was this warning given?
  C. Peter warns, "Therefore, brethren, be even more diligent to make your call and election sure, for if you do these things you will never stumble" (2 Pet. 1:10).
    1. If a Christian cannot stumble and fall away, why was this warning given to Christians?

IV. **The Bible Gives Numerous _____ of Those Who Did Fall Away and Lose Their Salvation!**
  A. Judas, one of the apostles, "fell away" (Acts 1:25, ASV) and he was "lost" (John 17:12).
  B. A congregation had "left [its] first love" and "fallen," and Christ was going to "remove" them and their right to "the tree of life," if they did not "repent" (Rev. 2:1-7; 1:20).
  C. Hymenaeus and Alexander had been "delivered to Satan," because they "rejected" the faith and "suffered shipwreck in regard to their faith" (1 Tim. 1:18-20).
  D. Hymenaeus and Philetus "strayed concerned the truth" (2 Tim. 2:17-18).
  E. Simon the sorcerer, after becoming a Christian, behaved in such a way that his "heart [was] not right in the sight of God," he needed to "repent" and be forgiven (Acts 8:9-24).
  F. If a Christian cannot fall away and lose his salvation, then these examples are deceptive.

V. **The Bible Vividly _____ That Some Would Fall Away and Lose Their Salvation!**
  A. God not only said that one could fall away, He expressly said that some would fall away.
  B. God assured that Christ would not return "unless the falling away comes first" (2 Th. 2:3).
  C. Paul predicted that men would "draw away the disciples after themselves" (Acts 20:30).
  D. "Now the Spirit expressly says that in latter times some will depart from the faith, giving heed to deceiving spirits and doctrines of demons, speaking lies..." (1 Tim. 4:1-3).
  E. "For the time will come when they will not endure sound doctrine...and they will turn their ears away from the truth, and be turned aside to fables" (2 Tim. 4:3-4).
  F. If a Christian cannot fall away and lose his salvation, then these passages are senseless.

VI. **The Bible Offers Various _____ of Christians Falling Away and Losing Their Salvation!**
  A. Some Christians fall away because of a lack of faith (Heb. 3:12).
  B. Some Christians fall away because of the deceitfulness of sin (Heb. 3:13).
  C. Some Christians fall away because of lusts and pride (1 John 2:15-17).
  D. Some Christians fall away because of persecution (Matt. 13:20-21; 2 Tim. 3:12).
  E. Some Christians fall away because of the cares, riches and pleasures of life (Luke 8:14).

F. Some Christians fall away because of the deceitfulness of riches (1 Tim. 6:9-10; Mk. 4:19).

G. Some Christians fall away because of false teachers/teaching (Ac. 20:29-30; 2 Tim. 4:3-4).

H. Some Christians fall away because they fail to grow as they should (Heb. 2:3; 5:11-14).

I. Some Christians fall away because they do not count the cost (Luke 14:28-30).

J. Some Christians fall away because they underestimate the devil (1 Pet. 5:8-9).

K. Some Christians fall away because they revert back to their old ways (Acts 8:9-24).

L. Some Christians fall away because they revert back to an old religion (Gal. 5:4).

M. Some Christians fall away because they revert back to old friends (1 Cor. 15:33).

VII. The Bible Clearly Depicts the _____ of Those Who Have Fallen Away!

A. The one who falls away has wandered "from the truth" to "the error of his way" and is in danger of ultimate "death" (Jas. 5:19-20).

B. For the one who falls away, it "has become worse for them than the first" (2 Pet. 2:20).

C. For the one who falls away, "it would have been better for them not to have known the way of righteousness, than having known it, to turn from the holy commandment (2:21).

D. For the one who falls away, it is like when "a dog returns to his own vomit," and when "a sow, having washed, returns to wallowing in the mire" (2 Pet. 2:22).

E. The one who falls away has "a certain fearful expectation of judgment" (Heb. 10:27).

F. The one who falls away is subject to a "much worse punishment" than those who "rejected Moses' law" and died "without mercy" (Heb. 10:28-29).

G. The one who falls away has "trampled the Son of God underfoot, counted the blood of the covenant…a common thing, and insulted the Spirit of grace" (Heb. 10:29).

H. The one who falls away is subject to the "vengeance" of God (Heb. 10:30-31).

I. The one who falls away is one who did "shrink back to destruction" (Heb. 10:39).

J. The one who falls away was one of "his [master's] own servants," but because he was "wicked and lazy" in his service, he is "cast…into outer darkness" (Matt. 25:14, 26, 30).

K. The one who falls away will be cast "into the furnace of fire," where "there will be wailing and gnashing of teeth" (Matt. 13:40-42).

VIII. The Bible Lovingly Details How One Who Has Fallen Away Can _____!

A. One who has fallen away has wandered from God, rejected God's ways, turned to his own way and is subject to the eternal punishment of God's justice.

B. Yet, God's love still longs for His wayward child to return to Him and be saved.

1. Even when God's people refuse to obey, harden their necks and rebel against Him, He is still "ready to pardon, gracious and merciful, slow to anger" (Neh. 9:17).

2. Like the father of the prodigal, God is eager for his lost child to come home, will run to receive him back, will embrace him and restore him completely (Luke 15:11-32).

C. As God has conditions (a law of pardon) for alien sinner's to be saved, God has conditions (a second law of pardon) for those who have fallen away to be saved.

1. First, a wayward Christian must _____!

(a) Simon the sorcerer was told, "Repent…of this your wickedness" (Acts 8:22).

(b) The church in Ephesus was told, "Remember therefore from where you have fallen; repent and do the first works" (Rev. 2:5).

(c) To truly repent:

(1) One must have "a broken and a contrite heart" (Psa. 51:17).

(2) One must have true "godly sorrow" for his sin (2 Cor. 7:9-10; Rom. 2:4).

(3) One must renounce his sinfulness and return to God (Luke 15:18-21).

(4) One must reform his ways and practice righteousness (Rev. 2:5; 2 Cor. 5:11).

(5) One must "bear fruits worthy of repentance" (Matt. 3:8).

2. Second, a wayward Christian must _____!
   (a) Simon the sorcerer was told, "Repent...and pray God if perhaps the thought of your heart may be forgiven you" (Acts 8:22).
   (b) After David sinned against God with Bathsheba, he cried out to God, "Have mercy upon me...Blot out my transgressions. Wash me thoroughly from my iniquity, and cleanse me from my sin...Purge me...Wash me...Make me hear joy and gladness...Hide Your face from my sins...Blot out all my iniquities...Create in me a clean heart...Do not cast me away from Your presence...Restore to me the joy of Your salvation..." (Psa. 51:1-12). What an example! What a heart!
   (c) While prayer cannot save in God's first law of pardon (because the alien sinner is not God's child), prayer will save in God's second law of pardon for His lost child!
   (d) When we pray, our intercessor and advocate, Jesus, pleads our case to the Father (Heb. 7:24-25; 1 John 2:1-2; Heb. 2:17-18; 4:14-16).
3. Third, a wayward Christian must _____!
   (a) First, he must confess his sinfulness to God.
      (1) "If we confess our sins, He is faithful and just to forgive us our sins and to cleanse us from all unrighteousness" (1 John 1:9).
      (2) The prodigal returned to his father and acknowledged, "I have sinned against heaven and in your sight" (Luke 15:21).
      (3) David confessed, "I acknowledge my transgressions...Against You, You only, have I sinned, and done this evil in Your sight" (Psa. 51:3-4).
   (b) Second, he must confess his sinfulness to his brethren.
      (1) "Confess your trespasses to one another, and pray for one another" (Jas. 5:16).
      (2) Make a confession privately to those sinned against (cf. Matt. 5:23-24; 18:15).
      (3) Make a confession as public as the sin itself. If sinfulness is known by the church, confess sinfulness to the church.
      (4) Brethren need to pray for the one returning (Jas. 5:16; Acts 8:24; 1 John 5:16).
D. If a Christian cannot fall away and lose his salvation, why provide him a law of pardon?

IX. The Bible Unmistakably Portrays Falling Away As a Danger for Every Christian to Avoid!

A. God wants us to make sure that we "take heed lest [we] fall" (1 Cor. 10:12).
   1. It is possible for any Christian to fall away, if he does not take heed to God's Word!
B. God wants us to "be even more diligent to make [our] call and election sure" (2 Pet. 1:10).
   1. We make it sure by (1) adding the Christian graces to our faith (1:5-7); (2) abounding in the Christian graces (1:8); (3) giving "all" and "more" diligence (1:5, 10).
   2. When we make our call and election sure, we "will never stumble" (1:10-11).
   3. If we do not grow as instructed by the Lord, we will assuredly stumble and fall!
C. God wants us to make sure our names are in the Book of Life (Luke 10:20; Phil. 4:3).
   1. Only those with their names written in the Book of Life will enter heaven (Rev. 21:27).
   2. "Anyone not found written in the Book of Life" will be cast into hell (Rev. 20:15).
   3. It is possible (once written) to have your name blotted out (Ex. 32:33; Rev. 3:5).
   4. It is possible for any Christian to be blotted out, if he fails to live by God's laws.

X. Conclusion

A. God's Word repeatedly teaches and warns that a child of God can fall away and be lost.
B. If a saved person could not fall away, then thousands of verses would be meaningless.
C. Although a Christian may wander from the truth, God longs for them to return to Him.
D. God's Word provides clear instructions for remaining faithful and avoiding apostasy.
E. Only those faithful until death will enter heaven (Rev. 2:10)! Those who fall will not!

Lesson 14: Church Membership & Its Responsibilities

Fundamentals *of the* Faith

I. **Membership in the Local Church Is _____!**
   A. It is helpful to understand that the Bible uses the word "church" primarily in two senses.
      1. It is used in a "universal" sense, referring to all saved persons of all time in all places.
         (a) This is how Jesus used the word when He promised to build His church (Mt. 16:18).
      2. It is used in a "local" sense, referring to a group of Christians in a local community.
         (a) This is how the Bible used the word when Paul visited and wrote to specific congregations of the Lord's church (Acts 13:1; 14:23; 1 Cor. 1:2).
      3. See Lesson 4, Roman numeral V for more on this point.
   B. When baptized into Christ, a person is automatically "added" to the church (Acts 2:41, 47).
      1. This is the church "universal"—i.e., the body of Christ composed of all the saved.
      2. One is "baptized into one body" (1 Cor. 12:13), added by God to that body.
      3. The saved are in the church; the church is all the saved (Acts 2:47; Eph. 5:23).
      4. Membership in Christ's church is automatic upon one's conversion to Christ.
   C. Once converted, every Christian _____ become associated with a local congregation.
      1. In the book of Acts, the first converts of a city became an established local church.
      2. The local church was a group of Christians who were banded together to work and worship together in collectively serving the Lord.
      3. A Christian being a member of a local congregation was and is not optional.
         (a) The first Christians "were together" (Acts 2:42-46)—not separate or "at large."
         (b) When Saul, a Christian, came to Jerusalem, "he tried to join the disciples" (9:26).
         (c) Saul & Barnabas were among those "in the church at Antioch" (Acts 13:1; 11:26).
         (d) Phoebe was a "servant of the church in Cenchrea" (Rom. 16:1).
         (e) Onesimus was "one of you" – a member of the church in Colosse (Col. 4:9).
         (f) Paul emphasized that "the body is not one member but many" (1 Cor. 12:14).
         (g) The local church is "fitted and held together by what every joint supplies" (Eph. 4:16).
         (h) Each local church is to be properly organized, with elders from "among" each congregation overseeing and deacons serving (Acts 14:23; 20:28; Phil. 1:1).
         (i) There was no organization in the church higher than the local congregation.
         (j) Each local church assembled as a body to worship (Ac. 2:42; 20:7; 1 Cor. 11:17-23).
         (k) Why would God give specific purposes for the local church and why would He place such emphasis on the local church if membership was an optional matter?
            (1) Why would God emphasize each individual member if it was just optional?
            (2) Why would God organize the local church if it was just optional?
            (3) Why would God expect worshipers to assemble together if it was optional?
   D. The local church remains today a group of Christians who are banded together to work and worship together in collectively serving the Lord.
      1. There is no such thing, in the New Testament, as being a member "at large."
      2. God expects every Christian to be an active part of a local congregation of His church.
      3. The local congregation is God's only collective functioning unit to carry out His work.
   E. As with any divine organization, membership in the Lord's church has responsibilities!
      1. One cannot be a member of a local congregation with no responsibilities.
      2. When one is part of a family, there are responsibilities.
      3. When one is part of a kingdom, there are responsibilities.
      4. When one is part of a body, there are responsibilities.
      5. When one is part of an army, there are responsibilities.

II. **Each Church Member Is Responsible for Being an _____ of the Local Church!**
   A. Every Christian needs to "be ready for every good work," be "zealous for good works" and "be careful to maintain good works" (Tit. 2:14, 3:1, 8; cf. Eph. 2:10).
   B. This work is to be done cooperatively and collectively in the church (Eph. 4:16).
      1. "Every joint" and "every part" of the body must be working.
      2. Every part must be "joined and knit together" to the other parts and do its "share."
      3. Every part must be involved in "supplying," "working," "doing" and "edifying."
      4. When every part does the work, it "causes growth" of the whole body.
   C. God has a place and a function in His body for every member (1 Cor. 12:12-27; Rom 12:3-8).
      1. We must each find and utilize our "function" in the body to the glory of God!
      2. The health, maturity and growth of the Lord's church is dependent upon our personal and active involvement in the work.
      3. Like Jesus, we "must be about [our] Father's business" (Luke 2:49).
      4. Like Archippus and Timothy, we must "fulfill" our various responsibilities in the church and not leave them unfulfilled (Col. 4:17; 2 Tim. 4:5).

III. **Each Church Member Is Responsible for _____!**
   A. The Lord expects His children to worship Him (Matt. 4:10; John 4:23-24).
   B. The Lord expects His children to worship Him every Sunday (1 Cor. 16:1-2; Acts 20:7).
   C. The Lord expects His children to truly participate in every aspect of worship (Acts 2:42).
   D. The Lord expects His children not to "forsake the assembling together" (Heb. 10:24-26).
   E. There are many reasons why we should attend every service (list from Wendell Winkler):
      1. To show the Lord that we love Him and need Him (John 14:15).
      2. To maintain our spiritual fervor (Matt. 24:12; Psa. 122:1).
      3. To benefit from the association, teaching, prayers and spiritual communion (Ac. 2:42).
      4. To satisfy our spiritual appetites and to grow stronger (Matt. 5:6; 1 Pet. 2:2-3).
      5. To encourage brethren through our presence and participation (Heb. 10:24; Eph. 5:19).
      6. To avoid the example we would set by our absenteeism (Matt. 5:16; Rom. 14:13).
      7. To be where we want to be when the Lord comes (Mk. 13:32; Lk. 12:43; 2 Pet. 3:14).
      8. To prevent defiling or searing our consciences (Tit. 1:15; 1 Tim. 4:1-2; 1 Jn. 3:20-21).
      9. To be in subjection to the elders (Heb. 13:7, 17).
      10. To prevent backsliding (1 Cor. 11:20-30; 2 Pet. 2:20-22).
      11. To keep from sinning (Jas. 4:17).
      12. To be where Jesus is and meet with Him (Matt. 18:20; 26:29; cf. Ex. 19:17).
      13. To walk in the footsteps of the early church (Acts 2:42; 20:7; 1 Cor. 14:23).
      14. To help us put the kingdom of God and His righteousness first in our lives (Mt. 6:33).
      15. To demonstrate that we have offered our bodies as living sacrifices to God (Rom. 12:1).
      16. To keep from disobeying (Heb. 10:25).
      17. To help us to be faithful unto death (Rev. 2:10).
   F. We should see worship as something we *get* to do, not something we *have* to do!
      1. Worship is not merely about attendance but about wholehearted participation.
      2. Our hearts should long to worship God every week with great gladness (Psa. 122:1).
      3. When the church assembles, where else would a child of God want to be?
      4. We must not look to do *as little as we can*, but long to do *all that we can* for God!
      5. Some Christians see "going to church" as the major portion of their Christian responsibilities. However, it is only a part of what God expects of us.
   G. See Lesson 8 for more details on the avenues of New Testament worship.

IV. Each Church Member Is Responsible for Ministering to the _____!
  A. The Lord says that members of His body are "members of one another" (Rom. 12:4-5).
      1. That verse is also translated, "Each member belongs to all the others."
      2. There is a reciprocal relationship that exists between the members of Christ's body.
      3. We are literally responsible *to* each other and *for* each other in the sight of God.
  B. We are responsible for exhibiting Christian _____ toward one another.
      1. We are to "love one another" (John 13:34-35; 15:12; 1 Pet. 3:8; 4:8).
      2. We are to "give preference to one another" (Rom. 12:10; cf. Phil. 2:3-4; Eph. 5:21).
      3. We are to "be kindly affectionate to one another" (Rom. 12:10; Eph. 4:32).
      4. We are to have "compassion for one another" (1 Pet. 3:8; Rom. 12:16; 15:5).
      5. We are to "consider one another in order to stir up love and good works" (Heb. 10:24).
      6. We are to "bear with one another" (Eph. 4:2; Col. 3:13).
  C. We are responsible for engaging in Christian _____ toward one another.
      1. We are to have "fellowship with one another" (1 John 1:7; Rom. 15:7).
      2. We are to "be hospitable to one another" (1 Pet. 4:9; Heb. 13:1-2).
      3. We are to "edify" and "exhort one another" (1 Thess. 5:11; Heb. 3:13).
      4. We are to "comfort" and "encourage one another" (1 Thess. 4:18; Heb. 10:25).
      5. We are to "admonish one another" (Rom. 15:14; Col. 3:16).
      6. We are to "serve one another" through love (Gal. 5:13; 6:10; 1 Pet. 4:10).
      7. We are to "bear one another's burdens" (Gal. 6:2).
      8. We are to "forgive one another" (Eph. 4:32; Matt. 6:14-15).
      9. We are to "pray for one another" (Jas. 5:16).
  D. There is a mutual responsibility to look out for and "care for one another" (1 Cor. 12:25).
      1. "If one member suffers, all the members suffer with" him/her (1 Cor. 12:26).
      2. We "rejoice with those who rejoice, and weep with those who weep" (Rom. 12:15).
      3. We must "warn the unruly, comfort the fainthearted, uphold the weak" (1 Th. 5:14).
      4. We must look out for those who are weak and endeavor to restore them (Gal. 6:1),
          for we could "save a soul from death and cover a multitude of sins" (Jas. 5:19-20).

V. Each Church Member Is Responsible for Preserving the _____ of the Body!
  A. The Lord desires for His body to be united in doctrine and practice (Eph. 4:1-16).
      1. His desire is for there to be "no divisions" in His body (1 Cor. 1:10).
      2. His desire is for there to be "the unity of the Spirit in the bond of peace" (Eph. 4:3).
  B. The unity of the body of Christ depends on each member (Phil. 1:27-2:11; Rom. 12:18).
      1. We must be humble in our dealings with each other (Phil. 2:3-11; 1 Pet. 5:5).
      2. We must set the proper example & influence (Matt. 5:13-14; 1 Tim. 4:12; Rom. 14:13).
      3. We must be impartial in our treatment of each other (Jas. 2:1-9; 3:17; Acts 10:34-35).
      4. We must control our anger (Eph. 4:26-27), our selfishness (Jas. 3:17), our words (Jas.
          3:1-12), our urge to talk about others (1 Tim. 5:13; 1 Pet. 4:15), etc.
      5. We must settle disputes in God's prescribed manner (Matt. 18:15-20; 5:23-24).
  C. Preserving the unity of the body also involves preserving the purity of the body.
      1. While we all sin, if a member will not repent of his sins, his fellow members must act.
          (a) The Lord tells us to not have fellowship with brethren living in sin (1 Cor. 5:1-13).
          (b) The Lord tells us to withdraw from those who walk disorderly (2 Thess. 3:6-15).
          (c) The Lord tells us that we cannot allow sin to persist in the church (1 Cor. 5:1-7).
      2. Withdrawing fellowship is not done to "kick someone out" or to be unkind.
          (a) It is done as an action of love for the person and his soul (Heb. 12:5-11).
          (b) It is done to help create a sense of shame in his heart and life (2 Thess. 3:14).

        (c) It is done to help him to "be saved in the day of the Lord Jesus" (1 Cor. 5:5).

        (d) It is done to help preserve the purity of the whole church (1 Cor. 5:6-8).

        (e) It is done to help save the world from sin (1 Cor. 5:7-13).

    3. Even after withdrawing fellowship, we must urge repentance (2 Th. 3:15; Gal. 6:1).

VI. Each Church Member Is Responsible for _____!

  A. The commission of the Lord to His church is the commission of the Lord to each member.

    1. Each of us have a personal responsibility to:

      (a) "Preach the gospel" to lost souls around us in the world (Mark 16:15).

      (b) "Teach them to observe all things" that Jesus commanded (Matt. 28:19-29).

      (c) "Bear much fruit," that we may be disciples and God may be glorified (John 15:1-8).

    2. It is not merely the responsibility of the preacher or elders! It is our responsibility, too!

    3. We must not be ashamed of the gospel (Rom. 1:16), but teach it publicly and privately (Acts 20:20), with boldness and confidence (Acts 19:8; 28:31).

  B. The church is commissioned to teach the truth and defend the truth.

    1. Each of us have a personal responsibility to:

      (a) Defend the gospel (Phil. 1:16-17) and "contend earnestly for the faith" (Jude 3).

      (b) Ensure the church remains "the pillar and ground of the truth" (1 Tim. 3:15).

    2. Again, this is the responsibility of every member, not just the preacher or elders!

    3. To effectively defend the gospel:

      (a) We must have a good knowledge of the gospel (Eph. 5:17; 2 Pet. 1:5; 3:18).

      (b) We must have a true faith in the gospel (Rom. 1:16-17; 10:9-17; Heb. 11:6).

      (c) We must have a deep love for the gospel (2 Thess. 2:10; Psa. 119:47, 97, 127).

VII. Each Church Member Is Responsible for Respecting and Submitting to the Elders!

  A. The Lord set up His church to have no organizational structure higher than the local level.

  B. The Lord specified the qualifications and work of the men who would lead the local church.

    1. These men must meet the divine qualifications in 1 Timothy 3:1-7 and Titus 1:5-9.

    2. These men are responsible for overseeing, shepherding & protecting the congregation.

    3. These men are responsible to God for the spiritual welfare of the congregation.

    4. These men are called elders, overseers, shepherds and pastors. (See Lesson 6 for more.)

  C. Each member is responsible for humbly following the eldership, as they follow Christ.

    1. We must respect those men who are elders (1 Thess. 5:12).

    2. We must respect their God-given authority (Acts 20:38-32; 1 Tim. 3:5; Heb. 13:7, 17).

    3. We must respect their weighty responsibility as elders (Heb. 13:17).

    4. We must "esteem them very highly in love for their work's sake" (1 Thess. 5:13).

    5. We must emulate their faith (Heb. 13:7).

    6. We must submit to them and obey them (Heb. 13:17).

    7. We must make their work a joy and not a grief (Heb. 13:17).

    8. We must be slow & cautious with criticism and not receive accusations (1 Tim. 5:19-20).

  D. God put elders in place to watch for our souls. Let's have respect for God and His plan!

VIII. Conclusion

  A. Membership in the Lord's church is not optional!

  B. Every member is needed, so that the body can properly function and grow as designed!

  C. Every Christian must be an active member of a local congregation of the Lord's church!

  D. Every Christian must actively participate in the worship of the church, in the lives of the members, in the unity of the body and in the teaching and defending of the truth!

  E. Every Christian must respect & submit to the elders who shepherd his/her congregation!

  F. There are other responsibilities of members covered in Lessons 15, 16 and 17.

Lesson 15: The Christian Life

Fundamentals
of the Faith

I. **The Christian Life Is a _____.**
   A. When one is baptized, he is "born again" (John 3:3-5) or "born anew" (ASV).
      1. All sins have been forgiven and forgotten (Acts 2:38; Heb. 8:12).
      2. Upon baptism, "our old man was crucified with Him" (Rom. 6:6).
      3. As God's new creation, a Christian gets to "start over" and do it God's way.
   B. The Christian life is described as "a new and living way" (Heb. 10:20).
      1. Upon conversion to Christ, a Christian is to "walk in newness of life" (Rom. 6:4).
      2. "Therefore, if anyone is in Christ, he is a new creation" (2 Cor. 5:7).
   C. Everything about the Christian life is new—what a Christian thinks, says, does, wants, believes, etc.
      1. Being "a new creation" is not a drudgery to bemoan but a blessing to enjoy!

II. **The Christian Life Is a Life of _____.**
   A. The Christian life is sometimes described in the New Testament as a "run" (Heb. 12:2; 1 Cor. 9:24-27), and sometimes it is described as a "walk" (Eph. 4:1; 5:2, 8, 15; 1 John 1:7).
   B. Christians are exhorted to be "steadfast, immovable, always abounding in the work of the Lord" (1 Cor. 15:58).
   C. Faithfulness involves:
      1. "Continuing with the Lord" and "in the faith" (Acts 11:23; 14:22), and not stopping.
      2. "Finishing the race" and "finishing the work" (2 Tim. 4:7; John 4:34), and not quitting.
      3. "Enduring all things" (2 Tim. 2:3, 10, 12; Heb. 10:36; 12:1), and not giving up.
      4. "Looking forward" and "reaching forward" (2 Pet. 3:14; Phil. 3:13), and not backwards.
   D. Jesus used words like "strait," "narrow" and "difficult" to describe the Christian life (Matt. 7:14; Luke 13:24). He told us that there would be trials and troubles.
      1. Therefore, we must be "diligent" (Heb. 4:11; 11:6; 2 Pet. 1:5, 10).
      2. Therefore, we must exercise "perseverance" (Rom. 5:3-4; Jas. 5:11; 2 Pet. 1:6).
   E. Faithfulness is required until "the finish line" – "until death" (Rev. 2:10).

III. **The Christian Life Is a Life of _____.**
   A. Our God is holy, and He has called upon His people to be holy (1 Pet. 1:15-16).
   B. To be "holy" is to be "set apart *from* the world and *unto* Christ."
   C. Christians are not to "be conformed to this world" (Rom. 12:2).
   D. As "a holy nation," we've been called "out of darkness into His marvelous light" (1 Pet. 2:9).
   E. Therefore, we must "abstain from fleshly lusts which war against the soul" (1 Pet. 2:11).
      1. We must "come out from among them and be separate" (2 Cor. 6:17).
      2. We must perfect "holiness in the fear of God" (2 Cor. 7:1).
      3. We must "pursue...holiness, without which no one will see the Lord" (Heb. 12:14).
   F. Rather than look like the world and act like the world, Christians have been called out and set apart to look like Christ and act like Christ (Eph. 5:1; 4:32; 1 Cor. 11:1; Phil. 2:5).
      1. Christ is our perfect example of holiness—both in what He did...and did not do!
      2. Christ left "us an example, that [we] should follow His steps" (1 Pet. 2:21).

IV. **As Faithful Christians Pursuing Holiness, We Must _____.**
   A. There are changes that must take place in our lives when we become Christians.
      1. When a Christian has "put on the new man which was created according to God, in true righteousness and holiness," he must "put off the old man" (Eph. 2:20-24).
      2. When a Christian has been "called out of darkness," he must "cast off the works of darkness" (Rom. 13:12).

3. When a Christian has "put on the Lord Jesus Christ," he must "make no provision for the flesh, to fulfill its lusts" (Rom. 13:14).

B. While sin and unrighteousness are ever-present dangers in this life, a Christian must seek to live a life of "denying ungodliness and worldly lusts" (Tit. 2:11-12).

C. To emphasize how strongly God views this matter, He chose some very direct verbs in His instructions to His people regarding ungodliness and worldliness: "avoid" (1 Tim. 6:20; 2 Tim. 2:23; Tit. 3:9); "abstain from" (1 Thess. 4:3; 5:22; 1 Pet. 2:11); "put off" (Eph. 4:22; Col. 3:8, 9); "put to death" (Rom. 8:13; Col. 3:5); "shun" (2 Tim. 1:16); "deny" (Luke 9:23; Tit. 2:12); "crucify" (Gal. 2:20; 5:24; 6:14); "cast off" (Rom. 13:12); "turn away" (2 Tim. 3:5; 1 Pet. 3:11); etc.

D. Christians are instructed to "test all things" (1 Thess. 5:21). Determine good and evil.
   1. Then, "Hold fast to that which is good. Abstain from every form of evil" (5:21-22).

E. The "forms of evil" and the "fleshly lusts" from which we are to abstain are countless, but God does specify a number of them to avoid, to give us clear direction in life:

Revelry (Rom. 13:13)	Adultery (Gal. 5:19)	Deceit (Rom. 1:29)
Drunkenness (Rom. 13:13)	Fornication (Gal. 5:19)	Evil-mindedness (Rom. 1:29)
Lewdness (Rom. 13:13)	Uncleanness (Gal. 5:19)	Gossip (Rom. 1:29)
Lust (Rom. 13:13)	Idolatry (Gal. 5:20)	Backbiting (Rom. 1:30)
Strife (Rom. 13:13)	Sorcery (Gal. 5:20)	Violence (Rom. 1:30)
Envy (Rom. 13:13)	Hatred (Gal. 5:20)	Pride (Rom. 1:30)
Greediness (Eph. 4:19)	Contentions (Gal. 5:20)	Boasting (Rom. 1:30)
Lying (Eph. 4:25)	Jealousies (Gal. 5:20)	Inventing evil (Rom. 1:30)
Corrupt speech (Eph. 4:29)	Outbursts of wrath (5:20)	Disobey parents (Rom. 1:30)
Bitterness (Eph. 4:31)	Selfish ambitions (5:20)	Sexual immorality (Col. 3:5)
Wrath (Eph. 4:31)	Dissensions (Gal. 5:20)	Impurity (Col. 3:5)
Anger (Eph. 4:31)	Heresies (Gal. 5:20)	Evil desire (Col. 3:5)
Clamor (Eph. 4:31)	Murders (Gal. 5:20)	Covetousness (Col. 3:5)
Evil speaking (Eph. 4:31)	Filthiness (Eph. 5:4)	Blasphemy (Col. 3:8)
Malice (Eph. 4:31)	Foolish talking (Eph. 5:4)	Filthy language (Col. 3:8)
Homosexuality (1 Cor. 6:9)	Coarse jesting (Eph. 5:4)	Partiality (Jas. 2:9)
Stealing (1 Cor. 6:10)	Kidnapping (1 Tim. 1:10)	Lust of the flesh (1 Jn. 2:16)
Reviling (1 Cor. 6:10)	Perjury (1 Tim. 1:10)	Lust of the eyes (1 Jn. 2:16)
Extortion (1 Cor. 6:10)	Evil suspicions (1 Tim. 6:4)	Pride of life (1 Jn. 2:16)

   1. God did not attempt to provide an exhaustive list of every sin.
   2. In some cases, He used general terms like, "forms of evil" and "fleshly lusts."
   3. After listing several sins in Galatians 5, He then added, "and things like these" (5:21).

F. As Christians, who are pursuing holy lives, we must work diligently to "not let sin reign" (or even have a foothold) in our lives and make no provision for it (Rom. 6:11-13; 13:14).

V. As Faithful Christians Pursuing Holiness, We Must Possess Christ-Like _____.
A. Christians are urged, "Let this mind be in you which was also in Christ Jesus" (Phil. 2:5).
   1. One's mind (or heart or pattern-of-thought) needs to reflect that of Christ.
   2. One's mind (or heart or pattern-of-thought) is often exhibited in one's attitudes.
   3. "Attitude" is defined as "the way you think or feel about someone or something."

B. Controlling our attitudes begins with controlling our thoughts.
   1. Our inner thoughts often make us and define us (Prov. 4:23; 23:7).
   2. Our inner thoughts will be reflected in our outer life (Matt. 5:21-28; 15:18-20).
   3. Therefore, we must learn to capture & control our thoughts (2 Cor. 10:5; 1 Pet. 1:13).

C. When a Christian puts on Christ-like attitudes, he will certainly possess and exhibit:

Love (Gal. 5:22)   Honesty (Eph. 4:25)   Merciful (Matt. 5:7)
Joy (Gal. 5:22)   Tenderhearted (Eph. 4:32)   Purity (Matt. 5:8)
Peace (Gal. 5:22)   Forgiving (Eph. 4:32)   Peaceable (Jas. 3:17)
Longsuffering (Gal. 5:22)   Compassion (Col. 3:12)   Willing to yield (Jas. 3:17)
Kindness (Gal. 5:22)   Humility (Col. 3:12)   Impartiality (Jas. 3:17)
Goodness (Gal. 5:22)   Meekness (Col. 3:12)   Honorable (Phil. 4:8)
Faithfulness (Gal. 5:22)   Patience (Col. 3:13)   Just (Phil. 4:8)
Gentleness (Gal. 5:22)   Thankfulness (Col. 3:15)   Harmonious (1 Pet. 3:8)
Self-Control (Gal. 5:22)   Contentment (1 Tim. 6:6)   Sympathetic (1 Pet. 3:8)

D. "For as [a man] thinks in his heart, so is he" (Prov. 23:7)
1. The inward spirit of a man is seen only by God (1 Sam. 16:7; John 2:24-25).
2. But, the inward spirit is manifested in the outward attitudes (Prov. 4:23).
3. Let us, as Christians, work to ensure that our attitudes emulate our Savior (Phil. 2:5).
E. If we truly "set [our] minds on things above" (Col. 3:2), the rest of who we are will follow.

VI. As Faithful Christians Pursuing Holiness, We Must Behave with Christ-Like _____.
A. Christians are given clear instructions regarding their actions:
1. "Present your bodies a living sacrifice, holy, acceptable to God" (Rom. 12:1).
2. "If you love Me, keep My commandments" (John 14:15).
3. "But be doers of the word, and not hearers only, deceiving yourselves" (Jas. 1:22).
4. "And whatever you do in word or deed, do all in the name of the Lord Jesus" (Col. 3:17).
5. "...that you may become blameless and harmless, children of God..." (Phil. 2:15).
6. "But why do you call Me 'Lord, Lord,' and do not do the things which I say?" (Luke 6:46).
7. "Therefore, to him who knows to do good and does not do it, to him it is sin" (Jas. 4:17).
B. The New Testament has much to say about Christians engaging in Christ-like living.
1. The first four books of the New Testament teach about Jesus and His life.
2. The fifth book of the New Testament teaches about how to give your life to Jesus.
3. The last twenty-one books of the New Testament teach how to live your life for Jesus.
C. While it is impossible to list all that a Christian is "to do," there are two insightful and detailed passages to consider: The Sermon on the Mount (Matt. 5-7) and Romans 12.
D. Consider carefully and implement intently these instructions for life from Matthew 5-7:
1. "Let your light so shine before men..." (Matt. 5:16).
2. "First be reconciled to your brother, and then come and offer your gift" (5:24).
3. "Whoever slaps you on your right cheek, turn the other to him also" (5:39).
4. "Whoever compels you to go one mile, go with him two" (5:41).
5. "Love your enemies, bless those who curse you, do good to those who hate you, and pray for those who spitefully use you and persecute you" (5:44).
6. "Do not do your charitable deeds before men, to be seen by them" (6:1).
7. "In this manner, therefore, pray: Our Father in heaven..." (6:6-13).
8. "If you do not forgive men their trespasses, neither will your Father forgive..." (6:15).
9. "Lay up for yourselves treasures in heaven" (6:20).
10. "You cannot serve God and wealth [money, ESV]" (6:24, NASB).
11. "Do not worry about your life" (6:25).
12. "Seek first the kingdom of God and His righteousness" (6:33).
13. "Do not worry about tomorrow" (6:34).
14. "Ask, and it will be given to you; seek, and you will find; knock, and it will be..." (7:7).
15. "Whatever you want men to do to you, do also to them" (7:12).

16. "Enter by the narrow gate" (7:13-14).

17. "Beware of false prophets, who come to you in sheep's clothing…" (7:15).

18. "Not everyone who says to Me, 'Lord, Lord,' shall enter the kingdom of heaven, but he who does the will of My Father in heaven" (7:21).

19. "Whoever hears these sayings of Mine, and does them, I will liken him to a wise man" (7:24).

E. Consider carefully and implement intently these instructions for life from Romans 12:

1. "Let love be without hypocrisy [genuine, ESV]" (12:9).

2. "Abhor what is evil. Cling to what is good" (12:9).

3. "Be kindly affectionate to one another with brotherly love" (12:10).

4. "In honor giving preference to one another" (12:10).

5. "Outdo one another in showing honor" (12:10, ESV).

6. "Do not be slothful in zeal [diligence, NKJV]" (12:11, ESV).

7. "Be fervent in spirit" (12:11).

8. "Serve the Lord" (12:11).

9. "Rejoice in hope" (12:12).

10. "Be patient in tribulation" (12:12).

11. "Be constant in prayer" (12:12).

12. "Contribute to the needs of the saints" (12:13).

13. "Practice hospitality" (12:13).

14. "Bless those who persecute you; bless and do not curse" (12:14).

15. "Rejoice with those who rejoice" (12:15).

16. "Weep with those who weep" (12:15).

17. "Be of the same mind toward one another [Live in harmony, ESV]" (12:16).

18. "Do not set your mind on high things [haughty in mind, NASB]" (12:16).

19. "Associate with the humble [lowly, NASB]" (12:16).

20. "Do not be wise in your own opinion" (12:16).

21. "Repay no one evil for evil" (12:17).

22. "Give thought to do what is honorable [right, NASB] in the sight of all" (12:17, ESV).

23. "If it is possible, as much as depends on you, live peaceably with all men" (12:18).

24. "Beloved, do not avenge yourselves" (12:19).

25. "But rather give place to [the wrath of God, NASB]" (12:19).

26. "If your enemy is hungry, feed him; if he is thirsty, give him a drink" (12:20).

27. "Do not be overcome by evil, but overcome evil with good" (12:21).

F. There are certainly more things that a Christian "must do" than can be listed here.

1. In addition to the above, a Christian must teach the gospel to the lost, edify the brethren, restore the wayward, worship God, grow spiritually, study His Word, etc., etc.

2. See the lessons on "Church Membership and Its Responsibilities" and "Christian Growth" for further responsibilities of the Christian life.

VII. Conclusion

A. The Christian life is the best life on earth! It is the "more abundantly" life (John 10:10).

B. Every Christian is blessed to wear the name of Christ and must bring it glory (1 Pet. 4:16).

C. God is faithful and God is holy. He has called His people to be faithful and holy.

D. God abounds in His efforts toward us. We must long to abound in our efforts toward Him.

E. Let us draw closer to God every day, so that we hate what He hates (Psa. 97:10; 119:104).

F. Let us draw closer to God every day, so that we think the way Jesus would have us think.

G. Let us draw closer to God every day, so that we act the way Jesus would have us to act.

Lesson 16: Christian Growth

I. **God Expects and Commands Christians to** _____!

  A. It is imperative that every Christian grow spiritually.

    1. God uses a present tense imperative in 2 Peter 3:18 to emphasize: "Grow! Grow now! And, keep on growing!"

    2. God requires great effort on our part to grow fully in our Christian lives (2 Pet. 1:5-11): "Giving all diligence," we must "be even more diligent" (1:5, 10) to grow!

    3. God expects us to be "mature" and to "go on to maturity" (Heb. 5:14; 6:1).

      (a) We do this by having our spiritual "senses trained to discern good and evil" (5:14).

      (b) We do this by "growing up" into Christ to "no longer be children" (Eph. 4:14-15).

  B. Stagnation in Christian growth is not acceptable to God (Heb. 5:11-14).

    1. Some Christians grow "dull of hearing" and do not grow as they should (5:11-12).

    2. Some Christians remain "a babe" in their Christian development (5:13).

    3. Christians who do not grow are reprimanded in this passage. We should take note!

II. **Strong Christian Growth Comes from** _____ **Regularly!**

  A. One of the greatest joys and privileges of being a Christian, and an essential part of Christian growth, is letting God speak to us through His Word!

  B. A vital link exists between growing as a Christian and growing in knowledge.

    1. "Desire the pure milk of the word, that you may grow thereby" (1 Pet. 2:2).

    2. "So then faith comes by hearing, and hearing by the word of God" (Rom. 10:17).

    3. "...Those who hunger and thirst for righteousness...shall be filled" (Matt. 5:6).

  C. Genuine Christian growth requires _____ God's Word.

    1. God pronounced a blessing upon those who read and hear His Word (Rev. 1:3).

    2. God promised that, "when you read, you can understand" (Eph. 3:3-4).

  D. Genuine Christian growth requires _____ upon God's Word.

    1. In addition to reading, we must contemplate and reflect on God's precious words.

      (a) The blessed man finds "his delight is in the law of the Lord, and in His law he meditates day and night" (Psa. 1:2).

      (b) Those who love the law of the Lord will make it their "meditation all the day," and even "awake through the night" to "meditate on Your word" (Psa. 119:97, 148).

    2. Meditation takes time, planning and effort, but the rewards are immense.

  E. Genuine Christian growth requires _____ God's Word.

    1. We must give ourselves to a diligent and regular study of God's Word.

      (a) "Be diligent (Study, KJV) to present yourself approved to God...accurately handling the word of truth" (2 Tim. 2:15, NASB).

    2. We must have the proper approach to our Bible Study.

      (a) Our study of God's Word must be eager (1 Pet. 2:2; Matt. 5:6; Prov. 2:1-6, 10).

      (b) Our study of God's Word must be a priority (Matt. 6:33).

      (c) Our study of God's Word must be diligent and regular (2 Pet. 1:5-6; Matt. 7:7).

      (d) Our study of God's Word must be full of love (Prov. 12:1; 2 Thess. 2:10-11).

      (e) Our study of God's Word must be reverent (2 Tim. 3:16; Neh. 8:5).

      (f) Our study of God's Word must be humble (Jer. 10:23; Matt. 7:7; Jas. 4:10).

      (g) Our study of God's Word must be thorough and honest (Acts 17:11; Psa. 119:160).

      (h) Our study of God's Word must be with understanding (Eph. 3:3-4; 5:17).

      (i) Our study of God's Word must be self-examining (2 Cor. 13:5; Acts 2:37).

      (j) Our study of God's Word must be patient (2 Pet. 1:5-11).

3. We must expand our personal library of tools for Bible study.
    (a) This should include multiple translations for comparison, concordance, dictionary, expository dictionary, atlas, sound commentaries, brotherhood periodicals, etc.
    (b) This should include computer software, websites and audio/video recordings.
4. We can use various methods in our Bible study.
    (a) We can study the Bible conventionally, by reading it from cover to cover.
    (b) We can study the Bible chronologically, by reading it in the order of actual events.
    (c) We can study the Bible topically, by investigating all that it teaches on a topic.
    (d) We can study the Bible devotionally, by using it for comfort, strength, hope, etc.
    (e) We can study the Bible systematically, by using a trustworthy study guide.
5. Whenever we study the Bible, we need to remember to read it slowly.
    (a) We often try to study the Bible too quickly or too methodically.
    (b) Slow down long enough to read each word and digest all that God has given to us.
F. Genuine Christian growth requires _____ God's Word.
    1. Don't let "memorizing" scare you. But, your mind has great power.
    2. Memorizing God's Word (or writing it on your heart) will benefit you:
        (a) When you are faced with temptations (Matt. 4:1-11; Psa. 119:11).
        (b) When you are sad, lonely or anxious (Psa. 100:1-5; 46:1-10).
        (c) When you are in need of direction and guidance (Psa. 119:105).
        (d) When you are called upon to give a defense for your faith (1 Pet. 3:15).
    3. Memorizing has various levels, all of which are useful:
        (a) You can memorize a verse word-for-word, along with its location.
        (b) You can memorize the "gist" of the verse, along with its location.
        (c) You can memorize the location of a verse that teaches/says a certain thing.
    4. Memorizing is not a test of your knowledge or intellect.
        Memorizing is a blessing to your faith and to your daily life as a Christian.
    5. When you really get into God's Word, God's Word will really get into you!
G. Set goals for your Bible study and identify specific steps to reach those goals.
    1. Set a goal to read the Bible for ___ (10?) minutes every day.
    2. Set a goal to meditate on the Bible for ___ (20?) minutes every week.
    3. Set a goal to study the Bible for ___ (30?) minutes every week.
    4. Set a goal to memorize ___ (1-2?) verse(s) every week or month.
    5. Set a place in your home as "the place where I read, meditate and study God's Word."
    6. If you won't miss a meal or won't forget your medicine, don't miss or forget your time with God and His Word. Do not let anything get in the way!

III. Strong Christian Growth Comes from _____ Regularly!

A. One of the greatest joys and privileges of being a Christian, and an essential part of Christian growth, is speaking to God through prayer!
    1. Reading Scripture allows God to talk to us. Praying allows us to talk to God.
    2. Praying allows us to draw closer to God (Jas. 4:8; 1 Pet. 5:7).
    3. Praying allows us to communicate with our Father, God and Creator (Heb. 4:16).
    4. Praying allows the heart to open up and express its desires to God (Rom. 10:1).
B. A special bond exists between the pray-er and God, for He will not hear everyone's prayer.
    1. The foundation of acceptable prayer is a Father-child relationship.
        (a) One must be a child of God to call upon Him as "Father" (Matt. 6:9).
        (b) One must be redeemed by Christ's blood to be His "child" (Eph. 1:7; Gal. 3:26-27).
        (c) One must continue to abide in Him and His Word to sustain that bond (Jn. 15:1-7).

2. From Scripture, we learn that God will only hear the prayers of:
    (a) Those who are His children (Matt. 6:9).
    (b) Those who are righteous (1 Pet. 3:12; Jas. 5:16).
    (c) Those who are obedient (1 John 3:22; Prov. 28:9).
    (d) Those who are holy (1 Tim. 2:8).
C. The wonderful privilege of prayer needs to consist of these elements to be acceptable:
    1. Praise and adoration of God, for who He is (Matt. 6:9).
    2. Thanksgiving to God, for everything He does and gives (Eph. 5:20; 1 Th. 5:18; Phil. 4:6-7).
    3. Confession of personal struggles and sins (1 John 1:9; Luke 18:13).
    4. Supplication, petition and request for personal needs (Matt. 7:7-11; Phil. 4:6-7).
    5. Intercession on behalf of others (1 Tim. 2:1-3; Phil. 1:3-4; Jas. 5:16; 1 John 5:16).
D. God wants us to pray in _____, about _____ and for _____.
    1. God wants us to pray in all situations.
        (a) "Pray without ceasing" (1 Thess. 5:17; cf. Rom. 12:12; Eph. 6:18).
        (b) "In every situation, by prayer...present your requests to God" (Phil. 4:6, NIV).
        (c) "Continue earnestly in prayer, being vigilant in it with thanksgiving" (Col. 4:2).
        (d) "Men always ought to pray and not lose heart" (Luke 18:1-5).
    2. God wants us to pray about all things.
        (a) "In everything...let your requests be made known to God" (Phil. 4:6).
        (b) Pray for the church and its unity (Matt. 6:10; John 17:20-21; Phil. 1:3-4).
        (c) Pray for physical, material needs (Matt. 6:11).
        (d) Pray for forgiveness (Matt. 6:12; 1 John 1:9).
        (e) Pray for strength in and deliverance from temptation (Matt. 6:13; 26:41).
        (f) Pray for wisdom and understanding (Jas. 1:5-7).
        (g) Pray for strength during personal struggles (2 Cor. 12:7-9; Matt. 26:39-44).
        (h) Pray for laborers to work in the vineyard of God (Matt. 9:38).
        (i) Pray for God's will to be done (Matt. 6:10; 26:39).
    3. God wants us to pray for all people.
        (a) Pray for "all people" (1 Tim. 2:1).
        (b) Pray for governing officials and rulers (1 Tim. 2:1-2).
        (c) Pray for "all the saints" (Eph. 6:18; Phil. 1:9-11).
        (d) "Pray for one another" (Jas. 5:14-16).
        (e) Pray for gospel preachers and their work (Col. 4:2-4; Eph. 6:18-19; 2 Thess. 3:1-2).
        (f) Pray for brethren who are struggling with sin (1 John 5:16).
        (g) Pray for the lost (Rom. 10:1).
        (h) Pray for our enemies (Matt. 5:44).
        (i) Pray for peace (Phil. 4:6-7; 1 Tim. 2:1-2).
E. The Bible makes it clear that praying to God has _____.
    1. We must pray to the Father (Matt. 6:9; Eph. 5:20), not someone or something else.
    2. We must pray in Jesus' name (John 14:13-14; Col. 3:17; 1 Tim. 2:5; Eph. 5:20).
    3. We must pray in faith (Jas. 1:5-7; Matt. 21:22), without doubting (1 Tim. 2:8).
    4. We must pray in accordance with God's will (1 John 5:14; Matt. 6:10; 26:39-42).
    5. We must pray while abiding in Christ and His Word, and vice versa (John 15:7).
    6. We must pray with the right motive and intent (Jas. 4:3; 1 John 3:22).
    7. We must pray with a humble heart (Jas. 4:6; Luke 18:9-14).
    8. We must pray with a forgiving spirit (Matt. 6:12-15; Jas. 5:15-16).
    9. We must pray fervently and sincerely (Jas. 5:16; 1 Th. 3:10; Mt. 7:7-11; Lk. 18:1-14).

F. The Bible makes it clear that praying to God has _____.
    1. We are promised that "the prayer of a righteous person has great power" (Jas. 5:16).
    2. We are permitted direct and bold access to the throne of God (Heb. 4:16; Eph. 2:18).
    3. We are assured that the Almighty God "hears us, whatever we ask" (1 John 5:14-15).
    4. We are promised that God answers our prayers (Matt. 7:7-11; Psa. 118:5).
        (a) Sometimes God answers by saying, "Yes" (Jas. 5:17).
        (b) Sometimes God answers by saying, "No" (Matt. 26:39-44; Heb. 5:7).
        (c) Sometimes God answers by saying, "Wait" (Jer. 42:4, 7).
        (d) Sometimes God answers by giving us something different (2 Cor. 12:7-9).
        (e) Sometimes God answers by giving us more than we ask (1 Kgs. 3:11, 13; Eph. 3:20).
    5. We are assured to "obtain mercy and find grace to help in time of need" (Heb. 4:16).
    6. We are granted a surpassing peace and heavenly protection (Phil. 4:6-7).
    7. We are given strength and power to withstand the devil (Eph. 6:13-18).
G. Set goals for your prayer life and identify specific steps to reach those goals.
    1. Set a goal to be in a constant mindset of prayer and communication with God.
    2. Set a goal to sit down and seriously pray at least once day.
    3. Set a goal to maintain a "prayer list" and pray for at least 5-10 minutes every day.

IV. Strong Christian Growth Comes from _____ Regularly!

A. One of the greatest joys and privileges of being a Christian, and an essential part of Christian growth, is gathering with brethren to study and to worship God together!
B. Have you ever seen a single stalk of wheat or a single blade of grass flourishing?
C. Personal, spiritual growth certainly requires personal and private time (see II and III).
D. But, God intended for true personal, spiritual growth to also incorporate brethren.
E. When brethren truly "edify" one another (1 Th. 5:11), they are building each other up.
F. When brethren study and worship together, they stimulate growth (Heb. 10:24-25).
G. A Christian cannot grow fully or properly without regular interaction with brethren!

V. Strong Christian Growth Comes from _____ Regularly!

A. One of the greatest joys and privileges of being a Christian, and an essential part of Christian growth, is personally teaching someone the gospel of Jesus Christ!
B. The growth that takes place in teaching the gospel is mutual growth.
    1. The one being taught is able to hear, learn and grow.
    2. The one teaching is able to study, learn and grow (and often more than the student).
C. Christians who are not growing are Christians who are not teaching (Heb. 5:12-14).
    1. Teachers are constantly studying to be ready to teach. This produces growth.
    2. Teachers are constantly asking God for help in teaching. This produces growth.
    3. Teachers, "by constant practice," "have their powers of discernment trained" (ESV).
D. The more you teach God's Word, the more you'll learn yourself, the more you'll know, the more you'll believe, the more you'll love, the more you'll grow, the more you'll teach!
    1. "Entrust these [things] to faithful men who will be able to teach others also" (2 Tim. 2:2).
    2. True, cedar-like strength of faith develops from teaching and defending truth.

VI. Conclusion

A. Like every loving Father, God wants His children to grow into mature, strong Christians!
B. Christian growth is not optional or ornamental, it is absolutely essential!
C. All Christians must give themselves diligently (not casually) to their growth as a Christian!
D. Your growth and strength as a Christian is directly proportional to all four ingredients: your Bible study, your prayer life, your assembling with brethren and your teaching frequency.
E. If you are not growing, examine these four areas. In which area are you falling short?

Lesson 17: Christian Stewardship

I. Being a Christian Steward Is a Fundamental Biblical Topic.
   A. First, it helps to define what "stewardship" is.
      1. The English word means "the conducting, supervising, or managing of something; the careful and responsible management of something entrusted to one's care."
      2. The emphasis is on responsible management of something that does not belong to you but belongs to someone else.
   B. The Parable of the Talents (Matt. 25:14-30) describes the Biblical emphasis of a steward.
      1. The owner/master "delivered <u>his</u> goods" to the workers/servants (25:14).
      2. Those entrusted with the master's goods were responsible for using and increasing.
      3. The principal amount and the increase all still belonged to the master, not the servant.
      4. The servants were held accountable for how they managed their owner's goods.

II. A Christian Steward Recognizes That All Things _____.
   A. A Christian knows that he does not own anything, but he is only a steward.
   B. ALL THINGS belong to God! There is nothing that is not God's!
      1. "The Lord made the heavens...the earth...and all that is in them" (Ex. 20:11; Gen. 1:1).
      2. "The earth is the Lord's, and all its fullness...and those who dwell therein" (Psa. 24:1).
      3. "'The silver is Mine, and the gold is Mine,' says the Lord of hosts" (Hag. 2:8).
      4. "For every beast of the forest is Mine, And the cattle on a thousand hills...If I were hungry, I would not tell you; For the world is Mine, and all its fullness" (Psa. 50:10-12).
   C. ALL BODIES belong to God!
      1. He created all of us, therefore, we belong to Him (Gen. 1:26; 2:7; John 1:3; Acts 17:28)! (a) Our very souls are His (Ezek. 18:4)! Our very purpose for living is His (Isa. 43:7).
      2. He bought us, therefore, we belong to Him (1 Cor. 6:19-20; 1 Pet. 1:18-19)!
   D. As hard as it is to accept and admit, nothing that we have actually belongs to us!

III. A Christian Steward Recognizes That All He Has _____.
   A. "<u>Every</u> good gift and <u>every</u> perfect gift is from above...from the Father" (Jas. 1:17).
   B. God gives man wisdom (Jas. 1:5).
   C. God gives man the skills and ability to figure things out (Isa. 28:23-29).
   D. God gives man the power to obtain wealth (Deut. 8:17-18).
   E. God gives man (and all creatures) life (Acts 17:25).
   F. God gives man all things. "And what do you have that you did not receive? Now if you did indeed receive it, why do you boast as if you had not received it?" (1 Cor. 4:7).

IV. A Christian Steward Recognizes That He Might Possess, But _____.
   A. The early church recognized that what they personally possessed was not actually their own.
      1. "...neither did anyone say that any of the things he possessed was his own" (Ac. 4:32).
   B. Since we are not the owners, stewards have only temporary control of some of God's gifts.
      1. "Naked I came from my mother's womb, And naked shall I return there. The Lord gave, and the Lord has taken away; Blessed be the name of the Lord" (Job 1:21).
      2. "For we brought nothing into this world, and it is certain we can carry nothing out" (1 Tim. 6:7).
   C. Since I do not own what I possess, I must be an especially diligent and careful steward!

V. A Christian Steward Recognizes That He Must _____ for His Stewardship.
   A. God is looking for and expecting faithfulness in His stewards (1 Cor. 4:1-2; Luke 16:10).
   B. God is going to come and "settle accounts with His servants" one day (Matt. 18:23-24).
   C. Each one of us will "give account of himself to God" (Rom. 14:11).

D. Each one of us will receive his due, "according to what he has done" (2 Cor. 5:10).
E. We will be required to give an account for how we've managed His gifts (Matt. 25:14-30).

VI. **A Christian Steward Will Carefully Manage His _____, Which Belongs to God.**

A. Christians are to "glorify God in your body and in your spirit, which are God's" (1 Cor. 6:20).
B. Christians are instructed to "present your bodies a living sacrifice..." (Rom. 12:1).
C. As an example for us today, the Christians in Macedonia "first gave themselves to the Lord" (2 Cor. 8:5). (Do we give with the same spirit that He gave to us?)
D. In properly managing the body and life that God has given to us, we must be:
1. Faithful stewards of our minds (2 Cor. 10:5; Prov. 4:23; Psa. 119:97; Phil. 4:8).
2. Faithful stewards of our mouths (Ps. 141:3; 35:28; Pro. 18:21; 21:23; Jas. 1:19; 3:1-12).
3. Faithful stewards of our eyes (Job 31:1; Prov. 23:31; John 4:35; Col. 3:1-2; 1 Jn. 2:16).
4. Faithful stewards of our ears (Psa. 81:13; Prov. 10:20; 23:22; Mark 4:9; Rev. 2:7, 29).
5. Faithful stewards of our hands (Ecc. 9:10; Rom. 12:11; Col. 3:23; Eph. 4:28; Gal. 6:10).
6. Faithful stewards of our feet (Prov. 5:8; 4:27; Jer. 35:15; Psa. 119:59; 1 John 1:7).
7. Faithful stewards of our hearts (Matt. 22:37; Prov. 23:26; Deut. 10:12).
8. Faithful stewards of our influence (Rom. 14:7; 1 Pet. 4:1-5; Matt. 5:16; 1 Tim. 4:12).
9. Faithful stewards of our will (Matt. 6:10; Luke 22:42; Rev. 22:17; John 7:17).

VII. **A Christian Steward Will Carefully Manage His _____, Which Belongs to God.**

A. As with all things, even our time belongs to God. As a gift from Him, we must use it wisely, knowing that we will give an account to Him for how we manage His time.
B. Time is an ever-passing commodity, which cannot be created or re-created.
1. The Bible speaks frequently about the passing of time (Job 14:1-2; 7:6-7; 9:25-26).
   (a) James summarizes it: "For what is your life? It is even a vapor that appears for a little time and then vanishes away" (Jas. 4:14).
2. The Bible speaks of using the time we have, for it is all we have (Matt. 6:33-34).
3. Time, once it has passed, "cannot be gathered up again" (2 Sam. 14:14).
4. We cannot create time, save time, rush time, slow time, borrow time, purchase time.
C. Therefore, every bit of time with which we are blessed must be used very wisely.
1. The brevity and uncertainty of life/time give added emphasis to its value and our responsibility toward it.
2. We must learn to "number our days, that we may gain a heart of wisdom" (Psa. 90:12).
3. We must learn to "walk circumspectly...redeeming the time" (Eph. 5:15-16).
4. We must learn to see all things in life as "but for a moment" (2 Cor. 4:17).
5. We must learn to make use of every "opportunity" we have to "do good" (Gal. 6:10).
D. Our time belongs to God! Let us use it for Him and His service!

VIII. **A Christian Steward Will Carefully Manage His _____, Which Belong to God.**

A. As with all things, even our talents, abilities and skills belong to God. As gifts from Him, we must use them wisely, knowing that we will give an account to Him for how we manage them.
B. All of our abilities and skills come from God.
1. We often think that our abilities, talents, skills and jobs belong to us—that we have developed them, honed them and made them what they are (leaving God out of it).
2. God does "freely give us all things" (Rom. 8:32).
3. "...In Him we live and move and have our being" (Acts 17:28).
4. In the first century, God imparted special spiritual gifts upon the early Christians.
   (a) "There are varieties of gifts...But one and the same Spirit works all these things, distributing to each one individually, as He wills" (1 Cor. 12:4, 11).
   (b) While these were spiritual gifts, the same must be true regarding our "natural" gifts.

5. The abilities that we have are blessings given to us directly from God.

C. Therefore, every ability and skill with which we are blessed must be used very wisely.

    1. "For everyone to whom much is given, from him much will be required" (Luke 12:48).

    2. "Whatever you do, do all to the glory of God" (1 Cor. 10:31).

    3. God asked Moses a question that ought to ring in our ears when considering what we have from the Lord to use for Him, "What is that in your hand?" (Ex. 4:2).

    4. The Parable of the Talents (Matt. 25:14-30) helps to put it into perspective.

        (a) God has given us gifts, "each according to his own ability" (25:15).

        (b) God expects us to be "faithful over" the things He has given us (25:21, 23).

        (c) God expects us to use them, develop them and increase them...for Him.

        (d) God will come to "settle accounts" with us, to see how we've used His gifts (25:19).

        (e) Even if we are not the most talented, able and skillful person (like the one-talent man), what we have has still been given to us by God and must be used wisely.

D. Our abilities, skills and talents belong to God! Let us use them for Him and His service!

IX. A Christian Steward Will Carefully Manage His _____, Which Belongs to God.

A. As with all things, even our money belongs to God. As a gift from Him, we must use it wisely, knowing that we will give an account to Him for how we manage His money.

    1. Whenever we talk about money, and especially when we talk about "giving," people get uncomfortable and sometimes even defensive.

    2. Let us remember that even "our" money belongs to God (Psa. 24:1; Hag. 2:8).

    3. Let us remember that Jesus "loved us" and gave "Himself for us, an offering and a sacrifice to God" (Eph. 5:2), so that we could be saved from our sins (Gal. 1:4).

    4. Let us remember that "the love of money is a root of all kinds of evil" (1 Tim. 6:10).

    5. Let us remember that working hard and earning money are expectations of God (2 Thess. 3:10; Eph. 4:28), and that "every gift" in our paycheck is from Him (Jas. 1:17).

    6. Let us remember that the Bible has more to say about giving than nearly any other topic.

B. Proper management of money involves making good choices.

    1. We must make good choices in how we "earn" our money and not engage in unlawful, ungodly, unethical, questionable means of "gaining" money.

    2. We must make good choices in how we "spend" our money and not be wasteful (prodigal), thoughtless and entirely selfish in how we disperse and use our money.

    3. We must make good choices in how we "invest" our money and not "gamble" God's money away in casinos, card games, betting on sports, lotteries, raffles, etc.

C. Proper management of money involves giving back to God what He has given to us.

    1. If we will "first give ourselves to the Lord" (cf. 2 Cor. 8:5), giving money will be easier!

    2. If we will give "our bodies a living sacrifice" (Rom. 12:2), giving money will be easier!

    3. If we will remember how much the Lord gave for us (Gal. 2:20), giving will be easier!

    4. If we will see our giving as a demonstration of our love (2 Cor. 8:8, 24), it will be easier!

D. God has instructed us in the _____ of our giving to Him.

    1. We need to give because He commanded us to do so (1 Cor. 16:1-2; 2 Cor. 9:6-7).

    2. We need to give as "the proof" of the "sincerity" of our love for Him (2 Cor. 8:8, 24).

    3. Giving is God's only means of supporting the needs of His church (1 Cor. 16:1-2; 9:14).

E. God has instructed us in the _____ of our giving to Him.

    1. A Christian steward is to give to God firstly (Prov. 3:9-10; Matt. 6:33; Mal. 3:7-10).

        (a) "Honor the Lord with your possessions, And with the firstfruits of all your increase."

        (b) God must not get "what's left"! He must get "what's right"! The first portion!

        (c) Before taxes, rent, cars, food, education, etc. comes God's first-sized portion!

2. A Christian steward is to give to God <u>regularly</u> (1 Cor. 16:1-2).
    (a) "On the first day of every week," one of the avenues of worship (every week) is giving to God. Therefore, this must be a priority and done weekly.
3. A Christian steward is to give to God <u>individually</u> (1 Cor. 16:1-2).
    (a) The instruction is, "...let each one of you."
    (b) Each one is responsible. No one can give to God for you or in your stead.
    (c) Each one is to bear/carry part of the load (2 Cor. 8:13-15; cf. Mark 12:41-44).
4. A Christian steward is to give to God <u>systematically</u> (1 Cor. 16:1-2).
    (a) Each Lord's day, Christians are to "put something aside and store it up."
    (b) The words here literally carry the idea of "putting into the treasury."
5. A Christian steward is to give to God <u>proportionally</u> (1 Cor. 16:1-2; cf. 2 Cor. 9:12).
    (a) A Christian is to give "as he may prosper," which includes every one of every class.
    (b) As God has prospered (and given to) each one, let that one give in return to God.
    (c) "...to whom much is given...much will be required" (Luke 12:48). What's "much"?
    (d) The more one makes, the more one must give (including raises, bonuses, tips, etc.).
6. A Christian steward is to give to God <u>liberally</u> (2 Cor. 8:1-4, 7; 9:6; Prov. 11:24-25).
    (a) God wants Christians to give liberally (Rom. 12:8), abundantly (2 Cor. 8:7), bountifully (2 Cor. 9:6). After all, He gave (and gives) in that exact manner to us!
    (b) Some in the Bible gave even beyond their ability (Mark 12:41-44; 2 Cor. 8:1-3).
7. A Christian steward is to give to God <u>purposefully</u> (2 Cor. 9:7; 8:10-15).
    (a) A Christian must "decide in his heart" (ESV) how much to give ahead of time.
    (b) Rather than giving haphazardly, we must pre-determine and make a commitment.
8. A Christian steward is to give to God <u>cheerfully</u> (2 Cor. 9:7; 8:12, 3).
    (a) A Christian must not give grudgingly, reluctantly or under compulsion (9:7).
    (b) There should first be a willing mind (8:12), which leads to a joy-filled heart longing (and eager) to express love and thanksgiving to God through giving.
9. A Christian steward is to give to God <u>sacrificially</u> (2 Cor. 8:1-7; Luke 21:1-4; Rom. 12:1).
    (a) God sacrificed His Son for us! Jesus sacrificed Himself for us!
    (b) Do we readily and truly sacrifice in our giving to Him? Not for our good, but His!

F. God has instructed us in the _____ of our giving to Him.
    1. "It is more blessed to give than to receive" (Acts 20:35).
    2. "Give, and it will be given to you..." (Luke 6:38, read the whole verse).
    3. "...All these things shall be added to you" (Matt. 6:33).
    4. "He who sows bountifully will also reap bountifully" (2 Cor. 9:6).
    5. "God is able to make all grace abound toward you..." (2 Cor. 9:8-12).
    6. Read Proverbs 3:9-10; 11:24-25; Malachi 3:8-10; Luke 18:28-30; 2 Chronicles 31:10-11.
G. Our money belongs to God! Let us use it for Him and His service!

X. **A Christian Steward Will Carefully Manage <u>the Gospel & Men's Souls</u>, Which Belong to God.**
    A. Christians are the "earthen vessels" entrusted with the saving gospel of Christ (2 Cor. 4:7).
    B. Christians know the value of the soul and its need for God's salvation (Matt. 10:28).
    C. Christians are responsible for converging the gospel with souls (Mark 16:15; Jas. 5:19-20).

XI. **Conclusion**
    A. All that we have belongs to God and has been entrusted to our care and management!
    B. God expects us to use, develop and increase all that He has bestowed upon us...for Him!
    C. Christians must be faithful stewards of their lives, time, abilities, money and the gospel!
    D. All Christians will give an account to God for how they have used His gifts to them!
    E. The manner in which we use His gifts is a demonstration of our love and devotion to Him!

Lesson 18: Marriage, Divorce & Remarriage

I. We Need to Appreciate Marriage As a _____!

A. Marriage was _____ by God, as detailed in Genesis 2.

   1. God created the man (2:7) and the woman (2:21-22), creating them for each other.

   2. God created marriage in the beginning, when "He brought her to the man" (2:22).

   3. Thus, it is God alone, not man, who has the right to govern all things marriage-related.

B. Marriage is _____ by God in His Word.

   1. Scripture gives "us all things that pertain to life and godliness" (2 Pet. 1:3).

   2. Marriage, by God's creation, incorporates both of these elements (life and godliness).

   3. As soon as God created marriage, He gave the principles to govern it (Gen. 2:24).

   4. Jesus used the same words, showing the timeless nature of God's regulation (Mt. 19:5).

   5. The Holy Spirit had Paul to quote the same principles again in Ephesians 5:22-33.

   6. Marriage has existed "from the beginning" (Mark 10:6), and so have God's laws.

C. Marriage is _____ by God in His Word.

   1. God's Word defines marriage as (adapted from Flavil Nichols):

     (a) The lifelong (Rom. 7:2-3)

     (b) Covenant (contract or commitment) (Rom. 7:2-3; Gen. 2:24)

     (c) According to the law of God (Mark 10:6-7)

     (d) And the laws of the land (Rom. 13:1-7; 1 Pet. 2:13)

     (e) Between two eligible persons (Mark 10:8)

     (f) Of opposite sex (one male and one female) (Gen. 1:26-27; 2:18-25)

     (g) Who become one with each other (Gen. 2:24; Mark 10:8)

     (h) With the privilege of sexual cohabitation (Gen. 2:25)

     (i) And the obligation to agape love one another (Eph. 5:22-33)

     (j) Until separated (disjoined) by death (Matt. 19:6; Rom. 7:2-3).

II. We Need to Understand _____ (The Only View That Matters)!

A. God gave the plan for marriage: the only plan that matters!

   1. Most conflict over MDR could be prevented & resolved if we'd learn & accept God's plan.

   2. God's plan today is the same plan He had at the beginning (Mark 10:6-9).

   3. God is the one who established the Divine and sacred relationship of marriage.

B. God gave the _____ for marriage.

   1. "From the beginning of the creation, God 'made them male and female'" (Mk. 10:6).

     (a) "Male and female He created them" (Gen. 1:27).

     (b) When God made a mate for the man, He created woman. That's God's plan!

   2. Monogamy (one male and one female) is authorized, not polygamy.

     (a) "…The two shall become…" (Mt. 19:5). There are only two—one man, one woman.

     (b) Spouses are always referred to as singular (1 Co. 7:2; 9:5; Eph. 5:23-33; 1 Pet. 3:1-7).

     (c) Jesus is married to the church, His one and only bride (Eph. 1:22-23; 4:4; 5:23-33).

   3. Heterosexuality (a male with a female) is authorized, not homosexuality, as specified throughout Scripture (Gen. 1:27; Mt. 19:4; Lev. 18:22; 20:13; Ro. 1:26-32; 1 Cor. 6:9).

     (a) Marriage, in God's eyes, is always between a man and a woman.

       (1) God joins a "man" to "his wife." He does not approve any other "union."

     (b) Every reference to homosexuality in Scripture is always a condemnation of the practice, without exception, for it defies God's design and definition of marriage.

     (c) Homosexuality is "against nature" (Ro. 1:26-27) and "strange" in God's eyes (Jude 7).

4. God, who alone can regulate marriage, restricts those who can enter marriage to:
   (a) A person who has never been married (1 Cor. 7:28; 9:5).
   (b) A person who has been married but whose spouse is dead (Ro. 7:2-3; 1 Cor. 7:39).
   (c) A person once married but whose spouse was put away for fornication (Mt. 19:9).
5. Of course, both parties in a marriage must be eligible in God's sight to marry.

C. God gave the _____ for marriage.
   1. The husband-wife bond is to take precedence over all other earthly relationships.
   2. This requires decisiveness – "a man shall leave his father and mother" (Gen. 2:24).
      (a) What was once a man's closest relationship must now yield to his marriage.
      (b) Loyalty to one's spouse must take precedence over loyalty to father or mother.
      (c) The man and woman must understand the importance of their decision.
   3. This requires commitment – "and shall cleave unto his wife" (Gen. 2:24)
      (a) "Cleave" = "to join fast together, to glue, cement," stick together no matter what!
      (b) This is an exclusive (between them alone) and continuing (until death) commitment.
   4. This requires unity – "and they shall become one flesh" (Gen. 2:24).
      (a) "One flesh" emphasizes a special kind of union between husband and wife:
         (1) The totalities of two lives are joined together into one life with one goal.
         (2) They become one physically, spiritually, emotionally, socially, psychologically, etc.
         (3) "This is now bone of my bones and flesh of my flesh" (Gen. 2:23).
      (b) For two to become one, each must surrender part of themselves.
         (1) "I"→"We" + "Me"→"Us" + "My"→"Our" + "Mine"→"Ours"
         (2) An "I, Me, My, Mine" must never take priority over "We, Us, Our, Ours."
   5. This requires exclusivity – "They were both naked, the man and his wife" (Gen. 2:25).
      (a) Husbands and wives must demonstrate absolute fidelity to each other.
   6. This requires a higher loyalty – "out of reverence for Christ" (Eph. 5:21, ESV).
      (a) The marriage relationship must share a mutual allegiance first to Jesus Christ!

D. God gave the provisos for marriage.
   1. There must be intention to live together as husband and wife (Matt. 19:5-6).
      (a) Leaving parents and cleaving to one's mate denotes an agreement to be married.
   2. There must be a commitment to each other (Gen. 2:24).
      (a) There must be a vow of devotion to each other, especially for spiritual purposes.
   3. There must be compliance with the laws of the land or the society in which one lives.
      (a) Christians must obey the laws of the land (Rom. 13:1-7).
      (b) Whatever the laws of the land require for marriage, Christians must comply
         (unless they violate the revealed will of God, which must come first—Acts 5:29).
   4. There must be love for and submission to one another (Eph. 5:22-25, 28; 1 Pet. 3:1).
      (a) *Agape* love must dominate the marriage & permeate all aspects of it (1 Co. 13:4-7).
      (b) Cohabitation does not equate to marriage (Heb. 13:4; John 4:18; Matt. 1:25).

E. God gave _____ to marriage.
   1. Marriage is to provide self-completion and wonderful companionship (Gen. 2:18).
      (a) It is not good to be alone; incomplete without the other; need one "comparable."
   2. Marriage is to enjoy sexual intimacy and fulfillment (Gen. 2:25; 1 Cor. 7:1-5; Heb. 13:4).
      (a) Marriage is the only divinely authorized situation for a man and woman to have sex.
      (b) Husbands & wives are "husband and wife" at the end of the marriage ceremony.
      (c) Each spouse has the exclusive right to the body of his/her mate, to be "one flesh."
   3. Marriage is to propagate the human race (Gen. 1:27-28).
      (a) God intended marriage to multiply a "godly offspring" (Mal. 2:15; cf. Deut. 6:7).

4. Marriage is to prevent or avoid fornication, sexual immorality (1 Cor. 7:2-4)
5. Marriage is to help each other get to heaven (1 Cor. 7:14, 16; 1 Pet. 3:1, 7).
6. Marriage is to provide an insight into Christ's relationship to the church (Eph. 5:22-33).
F. God gave _____ to marriage.
   1. God's general law of marriage is that it is for life (Mk. 10:9-12; Ro. 7:2-3; 1 Co. 7:10-11).
   2. From the beginning, marriage was to be a permanent bond.
      (a) "Leave father and mother" does not ever have returning in view. It's permanent!
      (b) "Cleave unto his wife" does not ever have "un-cleaving" in view. It's permanent!
      (c) "Shall become one flesh" does not ever have "two flesh" in view. It's permanent!
   3. Jesus emphatically affirmed the permanency of marriage.
      (a) Jesus contrasted the popular view of His day (end marriage for any reason).
      (b) Jesus taught "leaving," "cleaving" and two becoming "one flesh" (Matt. 19:5).
      (c) Jesus taught, "They are no longer two but one flesh" (Matt. 19:6).
      (d) Jesus taught, "God has joined together" AND "Let not man separate" (Mt. 19:6).
   4. God intended (and still intends) for marriage to last until death separates them.
      (a) God planned for marriage to be for life!
      (b) "The woman who has a husband is bound by the law to her husband as long as he lives. But if the husband dies, she is released from the law of her husband" (Ro. 7:2).
      (c) "A wife is bound by law as long as her husband lives" (1 Cor. 7:39).
      (d) Leaving, cleaving and weaving two lives together, in God's eyes, is irrevocable!

III. **We Need to Understand _____ in God's Eyes (The Only View That Matters)!**
   A. The N.T. Greek word for divorce is *apoluo.*
      1. It means "to set free, release; let go, send away, dismiss."
      2. It is often translated, "put away," involving a mental, intentional, then legal act.
   B. Marriage involves a contract/covenant between _____: man, woman, God.
      1. If marriage involves more than just the two human parties, then divorce also must involve more than just the two human parties.
      2. If the only marriages "acceptable" to God are ones He joins together, then, it would seem to follow that, the only divorces "acceptable" to God are ones He disjoins.
      3. If three parties are involved in proper marriages, One cannot be omitted during divorce. Only God can "join" and only God can "disjoin."
   C. God's plan for marriage (from the beginning) _____ included or intended _____ at all.
      1. From the beginning, God's design for marriage was for one man and one woman to become one flesh and remain together for one lifetime (Matt. 19:3-9).
      2. While there was a temporary "concession" ("permitting" and "suffering" divorce for a time) such was not commanded, required or desired by God. Hence, when Jesus came and taught on the matter, He restored God's original plan from the beginning.
      3. God's view of divorce is simple, yet strong – "He hates divorce" (Mal. 2:16)!
      4. For a spiritual understanding of God's view of violating marital fidelity, read Ezekiel 16.
   D. God's marriage laws are not bound, loosed or altered by what man approves or legislates.
      1. God's Divine law is not subservient to civil law! Ever!
         (a) We are to "submit...for the Lord's sake to every human institution" (1 Pet. 2:13).
         (b) But, when human law is not in harmony with Divine law, God's law trumps (Ac. 5:29).
         (c) Human/Civil law only has authority that God has provided it (Ro. 13:4; Jn. 19:11).
         (d) Human law has no power to *sanction a wrong* or *forbid something that's right.*
         (e) While civil law differs from culture to culture and will change even within a single culture, God's law remains constant and consistent.

2. If civil law joins two people together, that does not mean that God has joined them.
   (a) Just because a marriage is "legal" (to man) does not mean it is Scriptural (to God).
   (b) Just because two people marry does not mean they had a right to marry.
   (c) Herod "married" Herodias (legally), but it wasn't lawful in God's eyes (Mk. 6:17-18).
3. If civil law disjoins two people, that does not mean that God has disjoined them.
   (a) Just because a divorce is "legal" (to man) does not mean it is Scriptural (to God).
   (b) Just because a divorced person remarries does not mean he/she has a right to do it.
   E. God's general rule regarding marriage, divorce and remarriage is:
      1. "Whoever divorces and marries another commits adultery" (Mark 10:11-12).
      2. If one "marries another" while the spouse lives, he/she will be an adulterer/ess (Ro. 7:3).
      3. If one's spouse "does depart, let him/her remain unmarried or be reconciled" (1 Co. 7:11).
      4. If one's spouse "dies," he/she "is at liberty to be married" (1 Cor. 7:39).
      5. This was God's original plan for marriage – a lifelong commitment (cf. Mal. 2:16)!
      6. Therefore, the Divine rule is that a second marriage is not acceptable but is sinful!
      7. If no Divine exception, there could be NO divorce and remarriage without adultery.
      8. The ONLY Divine exception is a mate who puts away a mate for fornication (Mt. 19:9).
   F. God allows _____ exception to His general rule for MDR (Matt. 19:9; 5:31-32).
      1. If divorce was acceptable to God for any/every cause, then His laws are meaningless.
      2. In marriage, neither spouse has a God-given right to break their union to each other.
      3. The ONE exception that God permits to His general rule of "marriage for life, no divorce," is the intrusion of a third party that strikes at the heart of this God-ordained "one-flesh union" – i.e., when a spouse takes that "one flesh" outside the marriage.
      4. If one's spouse is guilty of fornication, God permits the innocent spouse to break the union and marry another without committing adultery. This is the only exception!

IV. We Need to Understand _____ in God's Eyes (The Only View That Matters)!
   A. Fornication is a broad term that includes all illicit sexual activity.
   B. The Greek *porneia* means, "every kind of unlawful sexual intercourse."
   C. It includes sex between unmarried people (1 Cor. 7:2), between individuals who may be married but not to each other (Matt. 19:9), homosexuality (Jude 7), bestiality, etc.

V. We Need to Understand _____ in God's Eyes (The Only View That Matters)!
   A. Adultery is a specific type of fornication—at least one party is married to someone else.
   B. The Greek *moicheia* means, "unlawful intercourse with the spouse of another."
   C. One can "live in adultery" (continuous sin) when God views the first marriage as still binding.

VI. We Need to Understand _____ in God's Eyes (The Only View That Matters)!
   A. Repentance, more than sorrow, is a "change of mind" that leads to "change of conduct."
   B. True repentance involves: [1] sorrow for sin (2 Cor. 7:10); [2] change of mind (Mt. 21:29); [3] change of conduct, including discontinuing sinful living (Matt. 3:8; 12:41; Acts 26:20).

VII. Conclusion
   A. In a day of disposable marriages and divorce "for every cause":
      1. God's Divine rule regarding MDR likely seems harsh to many (or most) folks.
      2. To hold to God's restrictive view of marriage can be unpopular and seem "unloving."
   B. The reaction of Jesus' disciples shows that God's view is intentionally narrow (Mt. 19:10).
   C. Rejection of God's marriage laws, leading one to engage in unscriptural divorces and remarriages, will cost that one (and any new "spouses") a home in heaven.
      1. "Fornicators and adulterers God will judge" (Heb. 13:4).
      2. "Neither fornicators...nor adulterers...will inherit the kingdom of God" (1 Cor. 6:9-10).
   D. Accept and follow God's view and God's laws of marriage, and you'll have no problems!

Lesson 19: The Work of the Holy Spirit

I. A Biblically Correct Understanding of the Holy Spirit Is Essential!

A. There is so much misunderstanding, misinformation and misleading about the Holy Spirit.

    1. Some view the Holy Spirit as some sort of mystical force, like a ghost or energy field.

    2. Some have created entire doctrines which demand a direct operation of the Holy Spirit upon the heart of an alien sinner, which is entirely without Biblical foundation.

    3. Some have become so confused that they avoid all study on the topic of the Spirit.

B. Christians need to know what the Bible teaches about the Holy Spirit!

    1. There are certainly some things that we do not know and cannot know (Deut. 29:29).

    2. But, where the Bible speaks, (1) we need to learn, and (2) we need to speak.

    3. In order to be able to defend against error on this topic, we need to know the truth!

C. We must study the truth about the Spirit, not as a reaction to error but as a desire for truth!

II. The Holy Spirit Is a _____!

A. The Holy Spirit is "a _____."

    1. The personal, masculine pronouns applied to the Holy Spirit show that He is "a person."

        (a) Jesus used seven personal pronouns for the Holy Spirit in John 16:13 alone.

        (b) The Holy Spirit is not an "it" or a mystical force. He is a "He."

    2. The works of the Holy Spirit proclaim that He is "a person."

        (a) Scripture teaches that He "speaks" (John 16:13; 1 Tim. 4:1), "testifies" (John 15:26), "teaches" and "stirs the memory" (John 14:26), "guides" (John 16:13), "leads" and "forbids" (Acts 16:6-7), "searches" (1 Cor. 2:10), etc.

        (b) A "thing" or an "influence" cannot do these things. Only a person can do them.

    3. The characteristics of the Holy Spirit verify that He is "a person."

        (a) He has a "mind" (Rom. 8:27), "knowledge" (1 Cor. 2:11), "affection" (Rom. 15:30), a "will" (1 Cor. 12:11), "goodness" (Neh. 9:20), etc.

        (b) A "thing" or an "influence" cannot have these things. Only a person can.

    4. The slights and injuries that He is able to suffer proves the Holy Spirit is "a person."

        (a) He can be "grieved" (Eph. 4:30; Isa. 63:10), "lied to" (Acts 5:3), "insulted" (Heb. 10:29), "blasphemed" (Matt. 12:31-32), "resisted" (Acts 7:51), etc.

        (b) A "thing" or "influence" cannot suffer such maltreatment. Only a person can.

B. The Holy Spirit is a "_____" person.

    1. The attributes of the Holy Spirit show that He is a "Divine" person.

        (a) He is "eternal" (Heb. 9:14), "omniscient" (1 Cor. 2:10-11), "omnipotent" (Mic. 3:8), "omnipresent" (Psa. 139:7-12). "The Holy Spirit" (Acts 5:3) is "God" (5:4).

        (b) Who but the Divine can possess such attributes?

    2. The works of the Holy Spirit indicate that He is a "Divine" person.

        (a) The Holy Spirit was at work in creation (Gen. 1:2; Job 26:13; 33:4; Ps. 33:6; 104:30).

        (b) The Holy Spirit is at work in regeneration (John 3:5; Tit. 3:5; Rom. 8:11).

        (c) The Holy Spirit is at work in providence (Psa. 104:30; Isa. 63:10-14; Acts 16:6-7).

        (d) The Holy Spirit was at work in the revelation and inspiration of the Holy Scriptures (Eph. 3:1-7; 1 Pet. 1:10-12; 2 Pet. 1:20-21).

        (e) The Holy Spirit was the source of the miraculous, when such was being practiced (Matt. 12:28; Acts 2:1-4ff; 1 Cor. 12:4-11; Heb. 2:1-4; 1 Cor. 13:8-10).

        (f) The Holy Spirit was the "another Comforter" whom the Father sent (John 14:16).

        (g) Who but the Divine can do such works?

C. The Holy Spirit is a Divine person "_____."
   1. The Bible teaches that there is a Godhead (Acts 17:29; Rom. 1:20; Col. 2:9).
   2. The Bible teaches that the Godhead is composed of three Divine persons—the Father, the Son and the Holy Spirit (Matt. 28:19; Rom. 15:30; 2 Cor. 13:14; Eph. 4:3-6).
   3. The Bible teaches that the three persons of the Godhead are separate and distinct (John 14:26; 16:13-15; Matt. 3:13-17), and that the Spirit is equally one of the three.

III. **The Holy Spirit Was Responsible for _____!**
   A. The Holy Spirit was operative in the revelation of God's Word to mankind.
      1. God's Word was revealed in words—an objective, understandable form of instruction.
      2. Note carefully that "prophecy never came by the will of man" (2 Pet. 1:21).
      3. Therefore, the words *always* came as inspired men "were moved by the Holy Spirit."
      4. David affirmed, "The Spirit of the Lord spoke by me, and His word was on my tongue" (2 Sam. 23:2; see also Acts 1:16). The words spoken were of the Holy Spirit.
      5. Jesus promised His apostles, "It will be given to you...what you should speak; for it is not you who speak, but the Spirit of your Father who speaks in you" (Mt. 10:19-20).
      6. The promises of the revelations of the Spirit in John 14-16 (remind, bear witness, teach, guide) applied to those inspired men in the first century and not to us today.
      7. God has revealed His Word and His wisdom "through His Spirit" (1 Cor. 2:10-13).
   B. The Holy Spirit was operative in the _____ (i.e., baptism) of the Spirit.
      1. The Spirit was promised to be poured out on all flesh, Jews and Gentiles (Matt. 3:11; John 1:33-34; Joel 2:28-32; Acts 2:17-21).
      2. There are only two recorded instances of Holy Spirit baptism (Acts 2 and Acts 10).
      3. In Acts 2, the apostles (Jews) were overwhelmed/baptized by the Holy Spirit:
         (a) To fulfill the promise of Jesus to His apostles (John 14:26; 16:13; Acts 1:4-5).
         (b) To empower them to perform miracles and impart miraculous gifts to Christians through the laying on of their hands (Acts 2:3-4, 6-8; 3:6-10; 4:7-10; 8:14-19).
      4. In Acts 10, the household of Cornelius (Gentiles) were baptized by the Holy Spirit:
         (a) To convince the Jews that the Gentiles had a right to salvation (10:44-48; 11:14-18).
      5. Peter affirmed that these were the only two instances of Spirit baptism (Ac. 11:15-17).
      6. Today there is only "one baptism" (Eph. 4:5).
         (a) Holy Spirit baptism was limited and temporary (and no longer occurring today).
         (b) Water baptism is the "one baptism," "even to the end of the age" (Mt. 28:18-20).
   C. The Holy Spirit was operative in the _____ of the Spirit in the first century.
      1. The apostles were empowered to impart miraculous gifts to Christians through the "laying on of the apostles' hands" (Acts 8:18; 6:6; 19:6; 2 Tim. 1:6).
      2. These miraculous gifts worked "signs" which were intended to "confirm" the spoken message (Mk. 16:20; Heb. 2:3-4)—power from God proving the message was from God.
      3. The duration of this measure of the Spirit (i.e., miraculous gifts) was limited:
         (a) It was limited to new revelations being confirmed. There are no new revelations from God today (Jude 3; 2 Pet. 1:3; 2 Tim. 3:16-17). Thus, this measure has ceased.
         (b) It was limited until the revelation of the N.T. was complete (1 Co. 13:8-13; Eph. 4:7-13). Now that the revelation of God is complete (Jude 3), this measure has ceased.
         (c) It was limited by the laying on of the apostles' hands (Acts 8:14-19). Since there are no apostles alive today (Acts 1:21-26), this measure has ceased.
   D. There is NO new revelation being made to any man today by the Holy Spirit!
      1. The revelation of God is complete (Jude 3; 2 Pet. 1:3; 2 Tim. 3:16-17).
      2. Therefore, the Word of God, in our Bibles, is the final and last revelation of the Spirit!

IV. The Holy Spirit Works in the _____!
- A. Denominational churches and preachers have twisted this doctrine.
  - 1. John Calvin taught "Irresistible Grace," in which the Holy Spirit's operation to convict the sinner, create faith and convert him to Christ is an act that cannot be "resisted."
  - 2. Some denominations have followed suit in emphasizing that "the Spirit called me" or "the Spirit showed me" or "the Spirit whispered to me" to "bring me to Christ."
  - 3. The question we must ask and answer is: What does the Bible say?
- B. The work of the Spirit in the conversion of a sinner to Christ is to _____.
  - 1. One cannot be converted to Christ without being convicted of sin (Acts 2:37-38).
  - 2. Jesus clearly identified "conviction" as the work of the Spirit in conversion (Jn. 16:7-8).
  - 3. So, the question remains: How does the Spirit convict a person of sin?
- C. The work of the Spirit in the conviction of the sinner is done _____.
  - 1. The Word of God is the product of the Holy Spirit, which is the means by which the Spirit operates. (Read 2 Samuel 23:2; Nehemiah 9:20+30; Acts 1:16; Mark 13:11.)
  - 2. "The Word" (i.e., the product of the Spirit and not the direct operation of the Spirit) is what generates faith in the heart of a sinner (Rom. 10:17).
  - 3. The only instrument wielded by the Holy Spirit is "the sword of the Spirit, which is the word of God" (Eph. 6:17); therefore, He will not operate by another means.
  - 4. The first converts "were cut to the heart"…"when they heard" the Word (Acts 2:37).
  - 5. If the Spirit were to operate outside or in addition to God's Word, it would prove that the Word is not all-sufficient (2 Tim. 3:17), complete (2 Pet. 1:3) and final (Jude 3).
- D. The work of the Spirit in the conversion of the sinner is done _____.
  - 1. The Word might "convict" someone, but that does not mean they are "converted."
    - (a) To be "converted" is a step beyond and above being "convicted."
    - (b) Again, through the Word is the only means by which He will operate on a sinner.
  - 2. The new birth requires two elements—"water and the Spirit" (John 3:5).
    - (a) "The Spirit" (John 3:5; Tit. 3:5) is shown to work through "the word" (Eph. 5:26).
    - (b) One is baptized into the body "by the Spirit" (1 Co. 12:13), or "the word" (Eph. 5:26).
    - (c) One is born again of "the Spirit" (John 3:5), through "the word" (1 Pet. 1:22-23).
    - (d) One is "washed, sanctified…by the Spirit" through "the gospel" (1 Cor. 6:11; 4:15).
- E. The work of the Spirit in the conviction of the sinner is _____ directly on the heart.
  - 1. If the Spirit works directly on the heart of the sinner separate from the Word:
    - (a) Then the Word is not all-sufficient, as it claims to be (2 Tim. 3:16-17; 2 Pet. 1:3).
    - (b) Then the gospel is not the power of God unto salvation (Rom. 1:16; Jas. 1:21).
    - (c) Then the preaching of the gospel is useless for conversion (1 Cor. 1:21).
    - (d) Then the mission of the church has no purpose toward salvation (Mk. 16:15-16).
    - (e) Then how does that account for people who are not convicted? Partiality? Failure?
  - 2. If the Spirit works directly on the heart of the sinner separate from the Word, why is there not a single record of such taking place in the New Testament?
- F. The work of the Spirit in the conviction and conversion of the sinner is tied directly to the effect that the Word of God has on the sinner's heart as he learns it and responds to it.
  - 1. It is irresponsible and without Scriptural authority to teach more or less than that!

V. The Holy Spirit Works in the _____!
- A. Different people respond differently to the idea of the Holy Spirit working in a Christian.
  - 1. Some embrace it and find joy in the thought of God taking a personal interest in them.
  - 2. Some go too far in thinking the Holy Spirit talks to them, nudges them and controls.
  - 3. Some avoid the idea all together and think the Spirit has nothing to do in/for them.

4. The question we must ask and answer again is: What does the Bible say?
B. The Bible teaches that the Holy Spirit _____ in every faithful Christian.
 1. The Bible teaches that the Father dwells in us (John 14:23; 1 John 4:12-16; Eph. 4:6).
 2. The Bible teaches that the Son dwells in us (Col. 1:27; 2 Cor. 13:5; Ro. 8:10; Eph. 3:17).
 3. Should it be so hard to believe that the Bible teaches that the Spirit also dwells in us?
  (a) In actuality, God dwells in us through His Spirit (Eph. 2:22; 1 John 3:24; 4:13).
 4. The Holy Spirit is given (as a "gift") "to those who obey Him" (Acts 5:32; 2:38).
 5. The Spirit "is in" the Christian, who is "the temple of the Holy Spirit" (1 Cor. 6:19-20).
 6. "The Spirit of God dwells in" faithful Christians (stated three times in Romans 8:9-11).
 7. Read also Galatians 4:6; 2 Timothy 1:14; 1 Thessalonians 4:8; 1 John 3:24; 4:13; etc.
C. The Bible teaches that the Holy Spirit's indwelling is _____ for the Christian.
 1. The indwelling confirms that a Christian is redeemed in Christ (Eph. 1:13; 4:30).
 2. The indwelling assures the Christian that he belongs to God (1 John 4:13; Rom. 8:9).
 3. The indwelling authenticates that a Christian is a child of God (Gal. 4:6; Rom. 8:14-17).
 4. The indwelling serves as a "guarantee of our inheritance" (Ep. 1:13-14; 2 Co. 1:22; 5:1-5).
 5. The indwelling motivates a Christian to "flee" from sin (1 Cor. 6:18-20; Rom. 8:9, 13).
D. The Bible teaches that the Holy Spirit's indwelling is in _____.
 1. The exact "how" of the Spirit's indwelling in the Christian is not revealed or known.
 2. The Spirit's indwelling must be in conjunction with the indwelling of the Word, for:
  (a) Christians are told that both are to "dwell" in and "fill" them (Eph. 5:18; Col. 3:16).
  (b) The work of the Spirit in a Christian cannot be outside of or separate from the Word,
       for God's Word is all-sufficient for the Christian life (2 Tim. 3:16-17; 2 Pet. 1:3).
  (c) The Spirit does not whisper in a Christian's ear or nudge him against his will.
 3. The Spirit's indwelling is not miraculous, for that age has passed (1 Cor. 13:8-13).
 4. The Spirit's working in the Christian is tied to the Word—exactly how is not known.
E. The Bible teaches that the Holy Spirit's indwelling imparts _____ to the Christian.
 1. Again, it must be emphasized that the exact manner of this working is unknown.
  (a) It must also be emphasized again the Spirit's work is connected to the Word.
  (b) It must also be emphasized that we must not venture where the Bible is silent.
  (c) It must also be emphasized that the Spirit is not some subjective, fuzzy "feeling."
 2. When God, through His Spirit (Eph. 2:22; 1 John 3:24), dwells in us:
  (a) He gives us "strength" (Eph. 3:16; Rom. 8:13), "love" (Rom. 5:5), "comfort" (Acts
       9:31), "hope" (Rom. 15:13), "peace and joy" (Rom. 14:17), but not miraculously.
  (b) He helps us to produce and bear the "fruit of the Spirit" (Gal. 5:22-23; cf. 5:16-25).
  (c) He "helps us in our weaknesses" and "makes intercession for us," when "we do
       not know what we should pray for as we ought" (Rom. 8:26-27; cf. Eph. 6:18).
 3. What a reassuring comfort to know that the Lord is working in us (Phil. 2:13)!

VI. Conclusion
A. There is much about the Holy Spirit and His work that we do not know!
B. We must not speak or suppose or wander into realms where God has given no revelation!
C. Nevertheless, where God has spoken, we must learn, teach and abide!
D. The Holy Spirit does not speak to us, move us or tell us what to do!
E. The Bible speaks to us, moves us and tells us what to do, for it is all-sufficient for the task!
F. How encouraging to know that as a Christian, we are not alone, but God is with us!
G. When it comes to the work of the Holy Spirit, may God help us to (1) speak only where
   the Bible speaks, and (2) live humbly and faithfully as "the temple of the Holy Spirit."
   (Helpful resources: Wendell Winkler's *The Holy Spirit: Questions Often Asked*; Wayne Jackson's ChristianCourier.com.)

Lesson 20: The Second Coming of Christ

Fundamentals of the Faith

I. **The Second Coming of Jesus Christ Is _____!**
   A. The second coming of Christ is a major subject of the New Testament.
      1. The Bible can be summarized in three sentences:
         (a) "Someone is coming" – the Old Testament.
         (b) "Someone is here" – Matthew, Mark, Luke and John.
         (c) "Someone is coming again" – Acts through Revelation.
      2. From the end of Jesus' life to the end of the N.T., the second coming is central theme.
   B. The second coming of Christ is an absolutely certain event.
      1. Jesus Himself promised it (John 14:1-3).
      2. The angels testified of it at Jesus' ascension (Acts 1:9-11).
      3. The apostles focused on it throughout their ministries (1 Thess. 4:13-5:11; Rev. 1:7).
      4. The resurrection of Christ guarantees His return (Acts 17:30-31).
   C. The second coming of Christ must take place as the culmination of God's eternal plan.
      1. God's whole scheme has been designed to unite His people with Him for eternity.
      2. Christ was sent the first time to save man, as part of God's eternal plan (1 Pet. 1:18-21).
      3. Christ will come the second time to usher in His eternal salvation (Heb. 5:9; 9:27-28).
      4. Christ is coming "to be glorified in His saints" and "admired" by believers (2 Th. 1:10).

II. **The Exact Time of the Second Coming of Christ Is _____!**
   A. Over the centuries, many have tried to predict the timing of Christ's coming.
      1. Some have done this because they misunderstood the "signs" in Matthew 24.
         (a) In short, regarding the "signs" in Matthew 24, Jesus taught, "This generation will by no means pass away till all these things take place" (Matt. 24:34).
         (b) All "signs" before verse 34 were pointing toward the destruction of Jerusalem in 70 A.D., which occurred in the lifetime of that "generation" to whom Jesus spoke.
      2. Many predictions of years and exact dates have been made, and every one failed.
   B. The Bible clearly teaches that the timing of Jesus' return is unknown by man.
      1. Jesus taught that "no one knows" the day and hour, "but My Father only" (Mt. 24:36).
      2. Jesus taught that He would return "at an hour you do not expect" (Luke 12:40).
      3. Jesus taught that the day would come as a thief in the night (Matt. 24:43; 1 Th. 5:2).
      4. Jesus taught that it is not for man "to know times or seasons" of the Father (Ac. 1:7).
      5. Jesus taught that man must "watch" because he does not know the time (Mt. 25:13).
   C. It is irresponsible and unscriptural to speculate as to a certain timing. We do not know!

III. **The Manner of the Second Coming of Christ Is Going to Be _____!**
   A. Jesus will come suddenly, without warning (1 Thess. 5:2; 2 Pet. 3:10; Matt. 24:36-44).
   B. Jesus will come personally and literally Himself ("this same Jesus") (Acts 1:11; 1 Th. 4:16).
   C. Jesus will come "in like manner" as He ascended (Acts 1:11).
   D. Jesus will come on a "cloud," "in the clouds," "with clouds" (Ac. 1:9; 1 Th. 4:17; Rev. 1:7).
   E. Jesus will come in such a way that "every eye will see Him" (Rev. 1:7).
   F. Jesus will come "in His glory" and "in the glory of His Father" (Matt. 25:31; Mark 8:38).
   G. Jesus will come with "all the holy [and mighty, 2 Th. 1:7] angels with Him" (Matt. 25:31).
   H. Jesus will come "from heaven with a shout" (1 Thess. 4:16).
   I. Jesus will come "with the voice of an archangel and with the trumpet of God" (1 Th. 4:16).
   J. Jesus will come "with all His saints" who "have fallen asleep" (1 Thess. 3:13; 4:13, 17).
   K. Jesus will come "to be glorified in His saints" (2 Thess. 1:10).
   L. There is no possible way that Jesus has already come, as some attempt to suggest.

IV. The Events of the Second Coming of Christ Will Be Overwhelmingly Spectacular!
  A. When Jesus returns, every dead person will be raised at the same time. (See V.)
  B. When Jesus returns, He will deliver the kingdom to His Father (1 Cor. 15:24).
  C. When Jesus returns, He will put "an end to all rule and all authority and power" (15:24).
  D. When Jesus returns, the earth and everything in it will be destroyed.
     1. Jesus foretold of the day when "heaven and earth will pass away" (Matt. 24:35).
     2. "The heavens will pass away with a great noise and the elements will melt" (2 Pet. 3:10).
     3. "Both the earth and the works that are in it will be burned up" (2 Pet. 3:10).
     4. "All...things will be dissolved" (2 Pet. 3:11; cf. Rev. 20:11; 21:1).
     5. The Bible does NOT teach that Jesus will reign on the earth for 1,000 years. When He returns, the earth will be destroyed and nothing will remain.
  E. When Jesus returns, every person who has ever lived will be judged. (See VI.)
  F. When Jesus returns, eternal destinies will be rewarded to all. (See VII.)
V. At the Second Coming of Christ, _____ at the Same Time!
  A. The doctrine of the resurrection is not a new idea introduced in the New Testament.
  B. The doctrine of the resurrection from the dead was known, believed and taught in the Old Testament (Job 19:25-26; Psa. 49:15; Dan. 12:2; Heb. 11:17-19).
  C. The doctrine of the resurrection is an "elementary principle of Christ" (Heb. 6:1-2).
  D. The doctrine of the resurrection was taught by Jesus (Matt. 22:29-32; John 5:28-29).
  E. The doctrine of the resurrection was central to the apostles' preaching (Ac. 4:2; 24:15).
  F. The resurrection of all the dead is guaranteed by the resurrection of Christ Himself.
     1. Christ "has become the firstfruits of those who have fallen asleep" (1 Cor. 15:20).
     2. Through Christ, and Him alone, has come "the resurrection of the dead" (15:21).
     3. "The last enemy that will be destroyed is death" (1 Cor. 15:26).
  G. The resurrection of the dead involves all of the dead, the righteous and the unrighteous, at _____.
     1. At His return, there will be a shout (1 Th. 4:16) and "the last trumpet" (1 Cor. 15:52).
     2. At the sound of "the last trumpet," "the dead will be raised" (1 Cor. 15:52).
     3. Simultaneously, "all...in the graves will hear His voice and come forth" (Jn. 5:28-29).
     4. "The sea...and Death and Hades delivered up the dead who were in them" (Rev. 20:13).
     5. In the "resurrection" (singular), "both the just and the unjust" will be raised (Ac. 24:15).
     6. Jesus emphasized the resurrection would take place on "the last day" (Jn. 6:40, 44, 54).
     7. There is no Bible verse that explicitly or implicitly teaches the premillennial doctrine of the righteous being raised first and then the unrighteous raised 1,000 years later.
     8. The Bible explicitly and repeatedly teaches that all will be raised at the same time.
  H. While all will be raised at the same time, the righteous and unrighteous will experience two very different resurrections.
     1. The righteous will "come forth...to the resurrection of life" (John 5:28-29).
        (a) Those who are "in Christ...shall be made alive" (1 Cor. 15:22).
        (b) Daniel prophesied that the righteous would "awake...to everlasting life" (12:2).
        (c) He whose "life is hidden with Christ...will appear with Him in glory" (Col. 3:3-4).
        (d) When raised, the righteous will receive incorruptible bodies (1 Cor. 15:41-45).
        (e) "We shall be like [Jesus]," "conformed to His glorious body" (1 Jn. 3:2; Phil. 3:20-21).
        (f) Those still alive will be caught up with them to meet the Lord in the air (1 Th. 4:17).
     2. The unrighteous will "come forth...to the resurrection of condemnation" (Jn. 5:29).
        (a) The unrighteous "shall awake...to shame and everlasting contempt" (Dan. 12:2).
        (b) Their resurrected bodies will be susceptible to pain and suffering (Mark 9:42-48).

VI. At the Second Coming of Christ, Every Person Who Has Ever Lived _____!

A. The day of judgment is a major theme of the Bible, in both Old and New Testaments.

B. The doctrine of "eternal judgment" is an "elementary principle of Christ" (Heb. 6:1-2).

C. The day of judgment is an "appointed" time for all men (Heb. 9:27).

D. The appointment of that day is guaranteed by Jesus' own resurrection (Acts 17:31).

E. When Jesus returns, He will sit on His throne of judgment (Matt. 25:31; Rev. 20:11).

F. Jesus will be the "Judge of the living and the dead" (Acts 10:42; 2 Tim. 4:1; John 5:22).

G. "All nations will be gathered before Him" (Matt. 25:32).

    1. "We must all appear before the judgment seat of Christ" (2 Cor. 5:10; Rom. 14:10).

    2. All of the living and all of the dead (small and great) will be judged (2 Ti. 4:1; Rev. 20:12).

    3. The righteous and the unrighteous will be judged by Him (Mt. 25:31-46; 2 Cor. 5:10).

H. Jesus has identified the standard of judgment as _____ (John 12:48).

    1. On the day of judgment, "books" (plural) will be opened (Rev. 20:12).

    2. One of the books that will be opened is the Book of Life (Rev. 20:12).

    3. The Word of God will be opened on that day and used to judge man (John 12:48).

    4. Every person will be judged "by the things...written in the books" (Rev. 20:12).

I. Jesus will separate the righteous from the unrighteous in the judgment.

    1. "He will separate [the nations] one from another, as a shepherd" (Matt. 25:32).

    2. This will not be arbitrary! All will be "judged according to their works" (Rev. 20:12).

    3. On that day, "each of us shall give account of himself to God" (Rom. 14:12).

    4. On that day, each one will "receive the things done in the body, according to what he has done, whether good or bad" (2 Cor. 5:10).

        (a) Each person's actions will be judged (Rev. 20:13; Matt. 16:27; Ecc. 11:9; 12:14).

        (b) Each person's words will be judged (Matt. 12:36-37; Jas. 3:1-12; Rev. 21:8).

        (c) Each person's thoughts will be judged (Ecc. 12:14; 1 Cor. 4:5; 2 Cor. 10:5).

        (d) Each person's response to the gospel (hearing, repenting, obeying) will be judged (Matt. 10:14-15; 11:20-25; 12:38-42; Rom. 2:3-11; 1 Pet. 4:17-18; 2 Th. 1:7-10).

        (e) Thankfully, no forgiven sin will be remembered against us (Heb. 8:12).

    5. The way one has lived (righteously or unrighteously) will determine his judgment.

J. Jesus, the Righteous Judge, will pronounce the final sentences on the day of judgment.

    1. The Judge will weigh a man's life against the standard of judgment, and then He will declare the final sentence.

    2. There are only two possible sentences that the Judge will issue on that day:

        (a) To the righteous (Matt. 25:23, 34):

            (1) "Well done, good and faithful servant; you have been faithful over a few things, I will make you ruler over many things. Enter into the joy of your lord."

            (2) "Come, you blessed of My Father, inherit the kingdom prepared for you from the foundation of the world."

        (b) To the unrighteous (Matt. 7:23; 25:41):

            (1) "I never knew you; depart from Me, you who practice lawlessness!"

            (2) "Depart from Me, you cursed, into the everlasting fire prepared for the devil and his angels."

K. Regardless of the sentence on that day, "Every knee shall bow to [the Lord], and every tongue shall confess to God" (Rom. 14:11).

    1. On that day, every person who has ever lived will be gathered before Christ.

    2. On that day, every person who has ever lived will give account of himself to God.

    3. On that day, every person who has ever lived will bow to and confess the Lord.

VII. At the Second Coming of Christ, _____ Will Be Rewarded to All!

    A. The second coming of Christ will be "the end" of many things (1 Cor. 15:24).
        1. It will be the end of this earth and all life and things on this earth (2 Pet. 3:10-13).
        2. It will be the end of opportunities to be saved from sin (2 Cor. 6:2; Heb. 3:12-15).
        3. It will be the end of the reign of Christ over His kingdom (1 Cor. 15:20-28).
    B. The second coming of Christ will be the beginning of eternity for all people.
        1. The unrighteous "will go away into eternal punishment" (Matt. 25:46).
        2. "The righteous" will go "into eternal life" (Matt. 25:46).
        3. The same word "eternal" (Greek, *aionios)* is used for both heaven and hell; therefore, just as one will last forever and ever, so equally will the other.
    C. The righteous shall be rewarded with eternity in _____.
        1. This is the eternal dwelling place of God (Matt. 5:16; 12:50; Rev. 3:12).
        2. This is the eternal & incorruptible inheritance for God's children (Heb. 9:15; 1 Pet. 1:4).
        3. This is the prepared, eternal home with many rooms (2 Cor. 5:1-8; John 14:1-3).
        4. This is the eternal rest from one's labors (Rev. 14:13; Heb. 4:9-10; 2 Thess. 1:7).
        5. This is the new dwelling place for God's saints & citizens (Rev. 21:1-4; Phil. 3:20-21).
        6. This is the abode where we will be present with the Lord forever (Rev. 22:1-5; 2 Co. 5:8).
        7. Only those written in the Lamb's Book of Life will enter, and no others (Rev. 21:27).
    D. The unrighteous shall be rewarded with eternity in _____.
        1. Just as heaven is a real, literal place, so hell is a real, literal place (Matt. 25:31-46).
        2. This is the eternal dwelling place of the devil and his angels (Matt. 25:41; Rev. 20:10).
        3. This is the lake (or furnace) of everlasting, unquenchable fire (Rev. 20:14-15; Matt. 13:42, 50; 25:41; Mark 9:43-48).
        4. This is the outer darkness or eternal blackness of darkness (Matt. 25:30; Jude 6).
        5. This is the chamber of torment, "day and night forever and ever" (Rev. 20:10; 14:11).
        6. This is the place of everlasting punishment away from God (Matt. 25:46; 2 Th. 1:9).
        7. Everyone not written in the Lamb's Book of Life will enter and remain (Rev. 20:15).

VIII. Every Person Needs to _____ for the Second Coming of Christ!

    A. God does not want any person to be lost (2 Pet. 3:9; 1 Tim. 2:4).
    B. God wants every person to spend eternity in heaven with Him (John 3:16; Rom. 5:8).
    C. Christ came the first time to save man from sins (Isa. 53:3-6; Mt. 1:21; Gal. 1:3-4; Jn. 3:17).
    D. Christ will come the second time to gather His saved to home in heaven (1 Thess. 4:17).
    E. At that moment, every person must be prepared to meet Him (Matt. 24:44) by:
        1. Bowing the knee before Him now and confessing Him as Lord now (Phil. 2:10-11).
        2. Working out his salvation with fear and trembling according to God's will (Phil. 2:12-13).
        3. Doing the will of the Father and obeying His commands (Matt. 7:21-23; Heb. 5:9).
        4. Enduring the trials and temptations of life and resisting sin in our lives (Jas. 1:2-21).
        5. Remaining faithful to the Lord and walking with Him every day (Rev. 2:10; 1 Jn. 1:7).
    F. If we neglect opportunities to obey, it will increase our guilt on that day (Matt. 11:20-24).

IX. Conclusion

    A. Jesus Christ is coming again the second time, but the day and hour are unknown!
    B. The second coming of Christ will be a great and glorious day of victory!
    C. The day of Christ's coming will be the last day on earth and the beginning of eternity!
    D. The eternal destinies of heaven and hell will be rewarded, based on one's life in Christ!
    E. There is no reason or excuse for us to be "caught off guard" at His coming (1 Thess. 5:4)!
    F. Christians should long for it and anticipate it with joyous expectation (Phil. 3:20; Tit. 2:13)!
    G. Now is the time to make the necessary decisions and preparations for that day (Mt. 24:44)!

Made in the USA
Columbia, SC
11 January 2022

54115616R00050